Advance Praise for *It's a Wonderful Afterlife*

"*Its' a Wonderful Afterlife* is an engaging and enlightening work that will assuage any doubts you may have that an afterlife exists. A gifted psychic medium, Kristy Robinett provides ample evidence from her own experience and the experiences of many others that not only is there a life after death but that those who have died can make themselves known, particularly to their living loved ones. You'll be hard pressed to put this book down once you start reading it!"

—Dr. Steven Farmer, author of *Healing Ancestral Karma*, *Earth Magic*, and *Animal Spirit Guides*

"From the minute I began reading *It's a Wonderful Afterlife*, I simply could not put it down. Like spiritual comfort food, Kristy's fluid command of the written word, coupled with her remarkable extrasensory abilities, makes for an inspiring experience. After reading Kristy's book, there is no doubt in my mind that life continues beyond the vale of death."

—Judith R. Burdick, MA, LLP, psychotherapist/ filmmaker, specializing in grief

"Kristy Robinett takes you on a metaphysical journey like no one else can. I get lost in her storytelling and am constantly amazed by her many gifts. She brings all of these talents to her latest offering in *It's a Wonderful Afterlife*. Once I started the book I could not put it down!"

—Allyson Martinek, Morning Radio Host— 963 WDVD; 963 WPLT and 963 WHYT

"A wonderfully written, insightful look at a world unknown and unseen by many. Filled with so many words of wisdom, messages of hope, and breathtaking stories that truly give a reader a new view on the mystifying life in front of them and that which lies beyond this world. A very personal reflection on a gift that can give readers a sense of faith and perspective on everything that happens around them."

—Kat DuBois, CBS Radio personality and journalist

"Another great release from Kristy Robinett! Her newest book gives us insight into the messages we receive from our deceased loved ones and is a wonderful portrayal of how we are connected to the other side. Her stories, which share not only personal readings but evidence of the afterlife, are uplifting, informative, and extraordinary. Get comfortable and be prepared to read it from start to finish!"

—Melanie Barnum, author of *Psychic Abilities for Beginners* and *The Book of Psychic Symbols*

"*It's a Wonderful Afterlife* is a beautifully written book that offers a fascinating glimpse of the Other Side."

—Leslie Rule, author of the bestselling book *Ghosts Among Us*

Disclaimer

Although the stories are based on real-life occurrences, some names and identifying details have been changed to protect the privacy of individuals.

To Write the Author

If you wish to contact the author or would like more information about this book, please write to the author in care of Llewellyn Worldwide, and we will forward your request. Both the author and publisher appreciate hearing from you and learning of your enjoyment of this book and how it has helped you. Llewellyn Worldwide cannot guarantee that every letter written to the author can be answered, but all will be forwarded. Please write to:

Kristy Robinett
℅ Llewellyn Worldwide
2143 Wooddale Drive
Woodbury, MN 55125-2989

Please enclose a self-addressed stamped envelope for reply, or $1.00 to cover costs. If outside the USA, enclose an international postal reply coupon.

It's a
Wonderful
Afterlife

Inspiring True Stories
from a Psychic Medium

KRISTY ROBINETT

Llewellyn Publications
Woodbury, Minnesota

FIRST EDITION
First Printing, 2015

Book design by Bob Gaul
Cover art: iStockphoto.com/43684280/©mashakotcur
         iStockphoto.com/40530588/©wiratgasem
Cover design by Ellen Lawson
Editing by Patti Frazee
Interior hummingbird illustration by Llewellyn Art Department

Llewellyn Publications is a registered trademark of Llewellyn Worldwide Ltd.

Library of Congress Cataloging-in-Publication Data
Robinett, Kristy.
  It's a wonderful afterlife: inspiring true stories from a psychic
medium/Kristy Robinett.—First Edition.
    pages cm
  Includes bibliographical references.
  ISBN 978-0-7387-4073-7
1. Future life. 2. Spiritualism. I. Title.
  BF1311.F8R63 2015
  133.9'1—dc23
                        2015003781

Llewellyn Worldwide does not participate in, endorse, or have any authority or responsibility concerning private business transactions between our authors and the public.

  All mail addressed to the author is forwarded but the publisher cannot, unless specifically instructed by the author, give out an address or phone number.

  Any Internet references contained in this work are current at publication time, but the publisher cannot guarantee that a specific location will continue to be maintained. Please refer to the publisher's website for links to authors' websites and other sources.

Llewellyn Publications
A Division of Llewellyn Worldwide Ltd.
2143 Woodale Drive
Woodbury, MN 55125-2989
www.llewellyn.com

Printed in the United States of America

Dedication

For all of those on the Other Side who have shared their stories and experiences with me. To those who have shown that they collect our tears when we weep. And those who collect our laughter like sun rays.

Contents

Acknowledgments

No one person can do it all, which has been a hard lesson for me to learn through the years. This book could not have happened without the thousands of clients and their loved ones on the Other Side who have touched my life more than I could ever eloquently communicate.

My love and appreciation first and foremost goes to my husband, Chuck Robinett, for his love and ice cream runs when I was stressing about deadlines. Thanks to my kids, Micaela Even Kempf and Connor Even, who have always understood my crazy job and schedule and even when I was feeling pressured and sassy, gave me hugs and a smile. To my step-daughters, Cora and Molly, for their love. To my dad, who makes me want to pull out my hair and hug him at the same time.

I am grateful for Mary Byberg, my assistant and friend, for her always upbeat attitude and for reminding me that glitter and sparkle can make any girl happy. And that we all have that glitter within us even when we think our glitter jar is empty.

I am thankful to Mike and Marjanna McClain for the late-night belly laughs and casino visits. Thank you to my mother-in-law, Mary Lou, for teaching me that tea should always be served in pretty teacups and that life is too short to listen to awful music.

I am grateful for my best friends and confidantes Gayle Buchan, Donna Shorkey, Laura Bohlman, and Jenni Licata. For Katie Eaves who gets me and who trusts me with her crazy entourage of ghosts. To Courtney Sierra for always making my hair look superb and for being the best and most affordable counselor a girl could ever have. Thanks to Lori Weiss for her love, support, and her constant questions, which make me do my own soul searches.

My thanks go out to my clients and my Facebook friends. My gratitude goes out to Llewellyn Publishing and my editors Amy, Stephanie, and Ed. Others that I am grateful for include Sheila Dever, Rosalyn Wrobel, Jennifer Hupke, Kass Hillard, Cheri Ford, Debbi Martone, Nancie Janitz, Deneen Baxter, and Caryn Gordon. Thank you to Team Afterlife: Deborah Bruno, Julie Ong, Jenny Thelen, Gloria Paulik, Melinda Kunst, and Tena Kuchar.

I am thankful to my own Spirit Guides for teaching me that learning and exploring never gets old, and that it doesn't necessarily have to take place in a classroom. And finally, to my mom in Heaven who reminds me that our loved ones on the Other Side are around us even when we don't feel them beside us, and that angels surround us during our happy times and during the darkest times.

Introduction

The Gift

My first taste of death came quite early. I was just three years old when an older lady came to me in spirit and told me to prepare my mom for her mom's passing. Being young and without a filter, I simply informed my mom that Grandma was going to die. The response I received was a spanking.

When my grandma passed just a few months later the so-called imaginary friends, as labeled by my family, I was seeing and communicating with became a bit truer and real. So when the next school year came my parents marched me up to the local Lutheran school at the age of four in hopes of eradicating whatever demons I might have been communicating with by replacing them with the Bible and busyness. That, however, didn't work. I still saw, heard, knew, and sensed, but instead of expressing that I saw life after death, I kept quiet and turned inward and shy. I was afraid of judgment and self-expression and tried to conform to what was perceived as normal, yet I felt that what I was seeing, sensing, knowing, and hearing *was* the normal.

My family saw a lot of death, mostly with my mom's side of the family. Freeman McLaughlin, my mom's oldest brother, passed from cancer before I was born. And then her youngest brother, Melvin, unexpectedly passed away from a heart attack when I was just a few years old, and soon after that my grandma passed. My mom's dad, Grant McLaughlin, was a gentle giant, soft-spoken, with a quick laugh and soft and caring blue eyes, and everyone who met him had an instant love for the man. He, however, did not have an easy childhood, and his adulthood gave way to many losses. After his sons passed away, and then his wife Helen, my grandfather became an even more notable fixture in our household, and a forever fixture in my heart.

It was at my grandpa's funeral, as his casket was being lowered next to his beloved wife, when I saw him standing next to a tree, smoking a cigarette. I ran toward him, thinking perhaps this was just a bad dream. Grandpa confirmed that he had passed on and was going to Heaven, but that he needed to let me know that he understood what I was going through because he, too, could see and sense. He told me that he would forever protect me and that I could call on him whenever I needed anything. With a final hug, which felt like I was hugging flesh and blood, he walked toward the big, old crooked pine tree where his earthly body lay, and disappeared. But not forever.

He would later appear in my dreams, and I now understand these weren't dreams at all, but visits. There would be
times when I would get goose bumps and then feel comforted, with a knowing that my grandpa was stopping in to
say hello. I would also smell stale cigarette smoke, and again
feel comforted that it was grandpa checking up on me. Even
when I tried to shut it all down, strange happenings—that
couldn't be mere coincidences—would continually occur.

It was only a few months after my grandpa's passing
when I visited a local mall with my mom and dad. I was only
eight years old and, well, not the clotheshorse that I am now.
So my dad accompanied my mom, with credit cards in tow
(as a form of therapy for her), as I sat on a gray concrete
bench in front of a large fountain—used as a wishing well
by kids and teenagers—with shiny pennies tossed into the
chlorinated water. It was only a couple of minutes before I
had my nose stuck into the newest book I was reading when
a man with a large camera around his neck came up to me
and asked if he could take my picture. I obliged, smiled, and
he snapped the photo. He asked me to stand up, noting that
the lighting wasn't right. I reluctantly stood up, smiled, and
again he snapped a photo. Before I knew it, he grabbed my
elbow and was steering me toward an exit, saying he needed
outdoor light to get an even better photo. What was probably mere seconds felt like hours and just as I began to panic, I
sensed my grandpa's energy around me. His large frame protected me just as he said he would. I could smell his cigarette
smoke and then heard in my ear his voice yell for me to run.

Without hesitation, I twirled away from the man, releasing the grasp he had on my arm, and ran as fast as I could toward the store where my mom and dad were shopping.

At that time, unbeknownst to me, an identified serial killer was haunting the area, kidnapping children and killing them. Now, we cannot say with certainty that this man was the serial killer, but he was not up to any good and my grandfather, the man who said he would protect me, more than likely saved my life all the way from the Other Side.

I was being taught in my parochial schooling that Heaven was some far-off place where you played musical instruments and sang in the choir. I liked doing both of those things, but the thought of being so far away from those I loved pained me—and especially after my experience with my grandfather, I didn't believe it.

It was reassuring for me to know that I was receiving the Heaven hellos, but my mom, who had lost her entire family, felt alone and sad. And although there were times I would try to share the hellos, she would cry, roll her eyes, or tell me to stop with my nonsense. But it wasn't nonsense.

After my grandma's crossing, it was as if the door to the Other Side wasn't just left open, but the door was ripped right off the hinges without an ability to shut it. This was to the chagrin of my Christian parents. The only person that never questioned what I saw, heard, felt, or knew, or made fun of me, was my mom's dad—my Grandpa Grant, the husband of the lady that I predicted would die. Instead there was a quiet understanding, something that continued even on the Other Side, and something that continues today.

It wouldn't be until I was close to thirty years old when I finally embraced what I had previously called a curse. I realized that it was truly a gift, and a gift that everyone has—that gift just needs to be recognized, unwrapped, and then used. I did the so-called normal thing of going to college, getting married, having kids, getting divorced, and then getting married again, but this time to someone who believed in all of me—including the gift. My new husband, Chuck, also had his experiences with family and friends that he had lost—experiences that weren't mere coincidences, but true signs.

Through doing sessions, group readings, radio shows, and even social media I've come to realize that we all need reassurance, and sometimes validation, that the Other Side is around us and it isn't our imagination or hopefulness. I've found that my so-called job is to be a messenger between worlds, bridging this side and the Other Side. It isn't necessarily about connecting all of the dots, but offering the dots and letting the dots connect over time. Sometimes the dots connect within the session; other times it is several weeks later. It isn't my job to give my clients the answers, but to allow them to have their own experiences. I can tell you that your mom is with you in spirit, and you may believe me, but you will also want some confirmation; I know that I do. Our loved ones want to offer that confirmation, but it comes in unique ways. Sometimes through nature, sometimes through numbers, and sometimes through smells, like the cigarette smoke from my grandpa.

Turning the Curse Into a Gift

I grew up being told time and time again that lack of action produced the exact same results; and although hoping was something to never stop doing, you had to back it with some wind. Much like a kite won't fly unless you throw it up and run, the same is true for your life—whether it is romantic aspirations or job goals, and anything in between. Doing things that feel painful or uncomfortable can just be part of the process.

In 2006 I was working at a corporate job during the day and doing sessions at a metaphysical center at night, undercover. Nobody other than Chuck and the kids knew what I was doing in the evenings. I even parked my car far away from the center so that nobody would see it in the lot. Chuck and I were not married yet, but it was inevitable that we would marry. Both Chuck and I love the sea air and the salt water, and even though Michigan offers us water (hello Great Lakes), it isn't the same as the ocean. So despite moans and groans from our kids, we packed up the car for a week's vacation in Solomon's Island, Maryland.

The cottage, which looked beautiful from the pictures posted online, instead looked like something out of a horror movie. State land surrounded us on one side and the Chesapeake Bay was on the other side. Thankfully the inside of the home was larger than it looked from the outside and it was comfortable, clean, and quaint. Although the kids were unhappy in the beginning, the trip was fun and it would become one of their favorite vacations.

It was our last day there when Chuck ran into town to grab some snacks for our ride home. The kids were all inside, lying in their rooms reading. I went out on the porch and sat in the rocker, staring off into the woods. I was sad to be leaving, but even more upset to have to go back to the nine-to-five job that I hated. I didn't just hate it; anytime I thought of going back my stomach hurt and I felt like it was slowly killing me. Tears sprung to my eyes and I quickly wiped them away, angry with myself for ruining the last day of vacation, thinking of the very thing I was escaping from.

"I don't know what I am supposed to do," I whispered into the wind. "I feel so lost!"

I suddenly heard a buzzing noise around me and thought at first it was a large bumblebee, but instead of a buzzing bee I realized that I was eye-to-eye with one of the most beautiful and magical creatures on this planet—a hummingbird. The hummingbird hovered in front of me for several seconds, unafraid, and slowly flew backward until the woods that camouflaged him and I lost sight of him. I knew that the hummingbird was a sign, but I had to connect all of the dots. After my magical encounter, I went inside and looked up on the computer what "hummingbird" meant in Animal Medicine. Here are what some of those websites note:

> The Native symbol for the hummingbird is about focusing on positivity. Hummingbirds are messengers of peace, healing, and they help guide through life's challenges. Hummingbird is filled with magic and love and wants

you to know that not everything is supposed to make sense. Hummingbirds can do what most birds can't, they hover, and the lesson when they show themselves is to hover on the situations before making any decisions, but decisions will ultimately have to be made.

A legend from the Kwakwaka'wakw says that Wild Woman of the Woods loved the hummingbird so much that she let him nest in her hair, but to others he looked just like a beautiful jeweled pin in her hair. Because these magical birds can hover, fly sideways, backward and forward, the message is that we are to look back to our past, but not to dwell on it, and to know that it is always best to move forward with the lessons and with the love, and savoring every sweet moment along the way. Native Americans also believe that hummingbirds show themselves before a positive event happens.

I pondered the encounter the entire ten-hour trip home. The attempted kidnapping and my encounters with spirits made me realize that my life purpose wasn't being fulfilled sitting in an office doing payroll and data entry. It was soon after my hummingbird encounter when I began assisting law enforcement agencies around the United States, helping on cold cases. My client load for life coaching, mediumship, and psychic sessions increased and I quit my real corporate job and did something really scary; I opened my own office to help connect this side to the Other Side.

Why Me?

I have been in many kitchens, living rooms, and police stations holding loved ones who had missing or murdered family members. I was able to share good news with some, but most often I was the closest thing to the Grim Reaper—and felt just like that more times than not. But there is a side other than just giving bad news, there is also explaining what the Other Side is like and how their child/father/mother/sister/brother are doing, or sometimes helping the loved one cross so that their soul can be content again.

"I just don't know if I can do this," I said, holding my head in my hands.

Chuck, my husband, sat looking at me helplessly. "Well …," he began, "why do you think you have this gift?"

"A punishment from something I did on a karmic level in a past lifetime?" I half joked. My eyes sparkled with fear and tears.

"Or that you are supposed to do things just like this to help," he said, ignoring my bad humor.

"Or that," I sighed.

Tommy was a ten-year-old freckle-faced little boy who came to me in spirit during a night visit. "I was killed on my way home from school. It was the neighbor who did it," he told me. So how was I going to tell a mom and dad that their son wasn't coming back to them? How was I going to tell them that it would be several months until the police would find his body and before they could put him to rest? And how was I going to…? There were more questions than answers, and although I was typically very good at winging it in certain situations, this wasn't one of them.

A knock on the passenger car window jolted me from my thoughts. The officer mouthed, "Ready?" to me and I nodded, even though I really just wanted to tell Chuck to hit the gas pedal and to drive me away from there.

I got through the awful meeting. I cried with the family and the officers. And I was there again several months later when their son's body was found in a wooded lot just a few blocks from his school. I helped them put the shell of their son to rest, knowing that they needed that closure, but also knowing that he had crossed months before. I did what didn't exactly feel comfortable, but in the end was the right thing.

So why me? Why was I given the gift, or what I called a curse for so many years? Well, it dawned on me as I transitioned between the terms "curse" and "gift" that it was neither of those. The ability to see, sense, hear, or feel those on the Other Side was something that everyone had; I was not extra special.

The sixth sense is a type of telephone system wired within each of us, but not everyone has called to have it turned on. Some need to turn the volume up, and yet others need to turn the volume down. Some are better at one technique, while someone else is better at another. Whether recognized or not, it is there. It isn't a super power and those that embrace it aren't extra special either. So why not me? And well, why not you?

There are several different kinds of abilities and by knowing the types, it helps to tune in, and sometimes tune out, loved ones on the Other Side.

Because of the constant clatter in our lives, it makes it difficult for us to hear from those physically around us. Parents, how many times have your children called for you before you finally heard and answered? Tuning out in order to tune in will help distinguish which sense you need to work on and then spend time to advance it. It is with practice that the trust and confidence comes forward so you don't think you are just making it all up.

There will always be skeptics and naysayers. It is not my job to prove to you or anyone else that life after death exists. I simply would like to share with you what I and others have encountered, in hopes that you find comfort in knowing that our loved ones surround us with love. And if we choose to invite them into our life, they can continue to be an intricate part of our—and their own—existence. They want to help us as much as they can and are capable of (which is actually more than you might think).

Even if you don't have a loved one on the Other Side, we all have Spirit Guides who act as our best friend from the Other Side, assisting in life's challenges and celebrations. Building and keeping that relationship intact is key. Just as relationships change with past coworkers when you move on to another job, or with family/friends when they move to another state, the same is true for those on the Other Side. You have to be proactive in building the relationship. It gets tiring to always be the one trying to initiate and secure that relationship, along with understanding and interpreting what signs and signals they give us when they are around. So spend some time talking, inviting, and loving. And although our loved ones have jobs on the Other Side, they are just a whisper away when you need them.

In the 1800s the term "hallucinations of the sane" was used to describe those who had encounters with the deceased. Waking dreams, whiffs of perfume or cigarette smoke, animal encounters…many people are merely frightened to admit they have had such an encounter for fear of being judged or laughed at. But it is real and true and it happens to both believer and skeptic.

I say it every single day in my office to my clients, you don't need a medium or a psychic to find your connection, you just need to tune out the world and then tune in and you will find your signs. You will then discover that it is a wonderful Afterlife.

Chapter One

Death and Dying

I've found over the years that many people are afraid of death until they are actually dying. Isn't it ironic that we come into this world crying and yet our bodies appear to be at peace when we depart? We mourn for those we've lost and yet those who've died rejoice that they've been set free.

When a person dies, their spirit and soul leave the physical body. For many, dying is a smooth transition going from one plane of existence to another. In many religions, the process is depicted as floating—the energy of the person departing from the physical and going to either a place of Heaven or Hell. Heaven, in many religions, is depicted upward and Hell as downward. This book, however, is not written to educate on the varying theological theories, but to instead share with you the stories and experiences I have received from the thousands of spirits that have communicated with me in my role as a medium. I don't claim to know everything. I don't.

With each soul that I speak with, I continue to learn. That is the journey of life, even after physical death.

My mom was dying and we all knew it, except for her. We attempted to keep hopeful and not share every detail of her health struggles with her as the doctors informed us in a play-by-play way. Our family was pretty much given a choice. Either my mom receive heart surgery, but she would probably die, or she didn't receive the surgery, and she would probably die. The odds weren't good. We didn't tell her the odds; instead, as a family we decided on the surgery with the hopes of a miracle. Several weeks later, she was moved out of the Critical Care Unit to a regular room. It made absolutely no sense to us as we knew that she wasn't non-critical, yet held on to the small strands of hope anyway. The medical staff removed her respirator and even gave her some soft food, something that she hadn't had in weeks. Her mood was happy, light, and she even had a youthful energy around her that the whole family noticed. I went to visit her one evening, by myself. Holding her hand, she whispered, "Kristy, I just want to go home."

"Mom, we are trying to get you there. I promise!" I answered, squeezing her hand, but she shook her head side to side.

"Not that home; *that* home," and she pointed over in the corner of her room where I could see several of her family members in spirit standing.

It wasn't a surprise when we received the call a day later that she had gone into cardiac arrest and passed away. My mom went home. Heaven is home.

Love Lives On

As the physical body stops, the soul and spirit leave the body. Sometimes the soul and spirit leave before the physical body has given out. There have been many who have felt the presence of their loved ones around them as they sat in the hospital room or waiting room, and sometimes even miles away from where their loved one is passing. And many who have had visits from their loved ones before they received the call of the death.

Natalie was sound asleep when she woke up to her dad sitting on the end of her bed. He had been taken to the hospital a few days previous for pneumonia, which wasn't good with his existing emphysema.

"Dad? How did you get home?" Natalie asked, confused.

"Shh…" Her dad responded. "I love you," he smiled and walked out of the room, but before she could follow him the phone rang. It was the hospital alerting her that her dad had just passed away.

"He said his goodbye to me," Natalie shared. "How beautiful and loving is that?"

On September 12, 2008, at 4:23 p.m. (PT), a Metrolink commuter train with 225 aboard slammed into a Union Pacific freight train on a winding route in the Chatsworth region of Los Angeles, California. Twenty-four people died and more than a hundred were injured. One of those who instantly died in the accident was Charles Peck. For hours after his death his family received over thirty phone calls from his cell phone;

there was no explanation about this from the phone carrier or the medical examiner.

Ben Breedlove was an eighteen-year-old from Austin, Texas, who posted several videos that went viral after posting a YouTube video titled "This Is My Story," announcing his rare heart condition. In his videos he shared that he cheated death three times, and in one of the videos he shared a story of being wheeled down a dark hall by nurses to the surgery room. Near the ceiling he could see a bright light that emitted a peaceful and calming energy. Through index cards that he showed the camera, he wrote, "There were no lights on in this hall. I couldn't take my eyes off it, and I couldn't help but smile. I had no worries at all, like nothing else in the world mattered. While I was still unconscious, I was in this white room; no walls, it just went on and on. There was no sound, but that same peaceful feeling I had when I was four. I was wearing a really nice suit, and so was my favorite rapper, Kid Cudi. I then looked at myself in the mirror—I was proud of myself, of my entire life, everything I had done. It was the best feeling. I didn't want to leave that place. I wish I never woke up."

On Christmas Day in 2011, one week after posting the videos, Ben Breedlove suffered a heart attack and died. At the funeral, his sister shared an interaction that she had with Ben after he collapsed and had a near-death experience just a few minutes before his final passing. She asked him if he was happy that he came back and he responded that he guessed, a response that shook her. Obviously, she and her family wanted Ben to survive and to have hope despite the dismal diagnosis.

"I think God let me feel that peace before I came back so that I knew Heaven was worth it," he told her.

The final two index cards in Ben's last video stated, "Do you believe in angels or God? I do."

Many spirits have told me that after they physically pass they look back over and see their body and take in where their passing happened and who might have been there. They can hear, see, and feel. They are often greeted by angels and their loved ones, who help them transition over to the Other Side. Some have described it like a stairwell, while others say it is like a tunnel with a bright light at the end of it. At the end of their trip down the pathway is a spiritual being filled with more love and peace than can ever be explained, but must be felt.

Sometimes during the transition the soul doesn't cross and they become lost between worlds, and wander until they find the light, or until they encounter someone who can help them cross over. The reasons why vary from violent deaths to unexpected accidents to mass deaths. Others are worried about what their eternal judgment might be and sometimes they want to make sure that their loved ones will be okay and are therefore afraid to take the final crossing.

See You Soon

It was the fall of 2011 when I woke up in the middle of the night hearing a ruckus in my kitchen where my makeshift office was set up. Thinking it was probably one of my pets getting into trouble, I reluctantly threw the blankets off of me, looked over at my husband who was peacefully sleeping, sighed, and made my way to see which cat or dog was the culprit. I was surprised when instead of one of my many pets, a man stood in the middle of my kitchen staring at my computer monitor, a monitor that I would always shut off every single night before I went to bed. The man looked real to me. He was over six feet tall with broad shoulders, in his late twenties to early thirties, and was dressed in pressed jeans and a collared blue shirt. For a split second I thought someone had broken into the house, and all I could say was, "Can I help you with something?" I think back to how silly that was to be polite to a possible house robber. Instead of looking to steal anything, the man pointed at the computer screen, to an article about a plane crash I had looked at earlier.

"So that's what happened to me?" the stranger asked.

It took a second for me to understand that this man had perished in that plane crash in another country. And someone that I had never met before was standing in the middle of my kitchen in Michigan. "I'm so sorry," I consoled.

The stranger introduced himself to me and then asked if I would tell his wife and kids that he loved them. "There's a note and the kids' most recent school pictures in the suitcase that I didn't take, in the closet."

I told him I wasn't an ambulance chaser. I couldn't, and wouldn't, just call up his wife and tell her that he appeared to me. He didn't seem too frazzled.

"Did you see a white light after the crash?" I asked him.

"I did. There were many of us just walking along the shoreline, confused why the people were diving into the water, because we weren't there. Or so we thought. I saw many people walk toward a tunnel of light, but I walked away and somehow found myself here," he said, his brow furling. Just as soon as the confusion set in and I was going to ask him how he thought he got from there to here, a look of peace and tranquility enveloped his entire body and he began to glow. He stared off and laughed, as if being part of a private joke. "I must go. My grandpa and my buddy tell me it's time." He took a few steps from my kitchen into the living room, turned around, and smiled at me. "Tell my wife I will see her soon," and then he disappeared.

I couldn't go back to sleep that night and didn't know what to do about his message, because what I told him was the truth; I refused to be an ambulance chaser. It ended up that I didn't need to be. A week later his wife called me for a session after hearing about me from a mutual friend. I was able to share the story of her husband in my kitchen, which made us both laugh even though we were both befuddled.

"He said that there was a note and photos in the suitcase in the closet, and that he would see you soon."

"Can you wait a second?" his wife asked. "Let me go check."

I heard the phone being set down and then heard a gasp. "Kristy, he wrote a letter to me and the kids. That was the note he meant. It's dated just a couple days before the crash. I wonder if he had a feeling his plane…" She didn't finish and broke down crying. "He never said goodbye, he always said *see you soon*. Always."

We all have those gut instincts, and yet don't know how to follow through on them. This man had to travel for his job. He was on a plane more than pilots were, but something made him write a recent letter to offer some sort of solace just in case.

Although his wife mourned for the loss of her handsome and talented husband, his "see you soon" offered her some comfort. She has since said he has visited her and the kids several times, both in their dreams and through signs.

Chapter Two

What Happens When We Die

What happens after the human body dies and the spirit leaves depends upon many different factors pertaining to how the death actually occurred. Was the person ill for a long time? Was the death self-inflicted or an accident? Was it the person's time, or were they stolen? It is rare for two people to have the same death experience just as it is rare for two people to have the same birth experience. Although there is a constant with regards to the spirit leaving the body and walking toward a light, some hear wind rustling, while others see varying colors. Some are alone on their walk down the tunnel, while others walk with family members or friends who had passed before them. My guides call the steps after the physical death the Heaven Chronicles.

The Heaven Chronicles

1. The Cross Over

   Once the physical body dies, the soul and spirit leave
   the body to take the journey to the Other Side. Some
   have described it as a long tunnel, others as a stairwell,
   and yet others as a doorway. Just as we have free will
   and free choice here on Earth, the free will continues
   to step into the unknown of the light.

2. The Soul Review

   A Soul Review, or Life Review, occurs after we
   cross over. This involves watching your life and
   all those people you've encountered and impacted,
   all the actions you've done—the good and bad.
   It is a teaching tool to understand that life, and
   death, is to be lived consciously.

3. Angel Boot Camp

   After the Soul Review you get to make decisions as to
   what is next. Some choose to quickly reincarnate and
   others decide to take time to reflect. Some decide to do
   what is called a soul split, which is leaving a piece of the
   soul in Heaven and incarnate another piece. Those that
   decide to stick around choose what their Heaven is and
   who it includes, as long as it coincides with the other
   souls. There aren't any clocks or time on the Other
   Side, but from an earthly plane explanation, this step
   takes six to twelve months, which is why I urge those

seeking an appointment with any medium to wait at least six months, but preferably twelve months after a person dies so that their loved ones are unpacked and settled, and can find their voice once more. After all, without a physical body, we don't have vocal cords to speak, right? We are also given an opportunity to help others. This may come in the means of being someone's Spirit Guide or a loved one's Guardian. It could also be an occupation in Heaven, but whatever it is, it's something that you choose and that you will love. You won't ever get that "do I really have to get up in the morning?" feeling here.

4. Living in Heaven

   If a soul hasn't reincarnated, then this is when living occurs—really living. You spend time with those you want to spend time with and do what makes you the most happy, with so much joy. Heaven exists all around the living. It isn't a place like we think of in the earthly sense. There is no physical world, instead it is the perfect world we imagine for ourselves. Whatever that perfect for you entails.

Afterlife Support

The group of six family members, three women and three men, sat in my small office, each one with their arms crossed in front of them in a defensive manner.

"Your mom just stepped forward with your dad, but your mom says she recently passed away, within the year, and your dad has been gone about five years."

The group silently nodded their heads confirming that was true.

"She shows me herself lying in a hospital bed, connected with tubes and machines. I feel the pokes of IVs in my arm," I said, touching my own arm as if it hurt. "She was there for many weeks and never came through. Her kidneys had failed," I said, looking away from their mom to them for validation only to be met with tears running down their faces.

"She says that you are mad at . . ." I looked to see who she was pointing to. "She says that you are mad at Julie for making the decision, but she made the right decision. Your mom was already gone. She was already with your dad at least a week before the machines were removed."

"So there wasn't any hope?" Jennifer, another of the sisters, asked.

I looked over at their mom, who held tight to their dad's hand and said that there wasn't. She was done fighting. "She says that Julie was the entrusted one with the medical decisions and ever since she made this one, well, you've blamed her for your mom's death. It had nothing to do with Julie."

Little by little the group unfolded their arms and with shame looked down at the floor—everyone except Julie, who looked at me and mouthed a thank you.

"Where do they live, Kristy? Where is Heaven?" Cal, one of the brothers, inquired.

"And she isn't in Hell, right?" Jennifer interrupted. "Taking her off of life support isn't like suicide, right?"

I could feel the tension quickly resume around the family. "No, she isn't in Hell." I listened to their mom's story and then offered it to them. "Heaven is a doorway to its own world in a higher dimension, but closer than we imagine. Although they don't have physical bodies, your loved ones can visit with you, and you with them; it is just different. Your dad says that since he got there first he chose their Heaven, and that he never got to choose anything!"

The group laughed.

"In all seriousness, though, your dad said that both he and your mom loved Florida and, after what they call a Soul Review and Angel Boot Camp, he moved on to a location much like their Florida experience. And your mom is happy and satisfied with it too."

"So it's an actual location?" Julie asked.

"Not really. It is more of that feeling. We don't have physical bodies and don't need physical things, but in order to explain it in our terms, they explain it in a physical way. So their Heaven is Florida."

"That would be my Hell," Cal joked. "I hate Florida!"

Everybody laughed.

When everyone was leaving, Julie leaned in and whispered, "Thanks for this. They've all been horribly angry at me and I have been mad, too, that Mom made me make this decision."

"No thanks necessary," I said as I hugged her. "Everything I said was true and came from your parents."

One of my many services is counseling those who are dying, those with family dying, and in turn those who have died, because believe it or not we carry our issues and regrets to the Other Side. The regrets seem to have a consistent theme. We all need to live on purpose rather than hold grudges and regrets for when we close our eyes to this world for the final time.

Life After Death

Just as each of us has our own unique birth story, our passing is just as unique. For those still left here, the pain and grief can be overwhelming. The missing of a loved one's voice, touch, and presence can be crushing. And the wondering if they are okay can lead to depression and constant worry. Did they hurt when they passed? Who did they meet when they crossed over? Will I ever see them again? Are they mad at me? Did I do the right thing? Could I have done more? These are just some of the questions that race through the mind of the mourner.

I went to a gallery reading, sometimes called a group reading, hosted by another medium, and each time she referenced "the dead," or "dead people," I shuddered. Our loved ones who made the transition aren't at all dead. Sure, they aren't with us in the physical, but they continue to be around us in some way, shape, or form—that butterfly that continues to flutter outside your window, or around you. The bird that follows you around the yard. The coins that you find on your walk.

The song on the radio that reminds you of someone special. The rainbow in the sky just as you were about to give up hope. Each one of us receives signs from our loved ones on the Other Side, but we often shrug it off as mere coincidence. There is an old adage that says, "Once is an accident, twice is a coincidence, three times is proof." The signs we receive show that our loved ones may have been taken from us in a physical way, but they aren't dead, and are actually alive, just in a different way.

Believing Is Seeing

For many people seeing is believing and unless they see with their own physical eyes, with visual evidence, it just doesn't exist. And yet if a bell rings and we don't see it, we still know that the bell rang. Scientists cannot see a black hole; they only observe what is going on and that determines there is a black hole, yet nothing is seen. And when the wind softly moves the tree branches, we don't question the wind. And so sometimes believing is seeing. It may just not be with your eyes but with your heart.

Everything is energy and according to the law of energy conservation and transmutation, energy can neither be created nor destroyed, but it can be manipulated to change form. So why, after the physical body stops working, wouldn't the energy of a person continue on in some way, shape, or form? So although the physical body is gone, the energy of their soul and spirit continue on with their personality, their memories, and quirks still intact. And it is the evidence that their loved ones on the Other Side give that helps turn a skeptic into a believer; however, an open mind and an open heart are needed.

Most scientists would state that the concept of an Afterlife is either nonsense, or unprovable. Yet, as science continues to advance and grow, so does the study of death and dying, and what exists beyond the grave. Some call this study quantum physics, while professor and author Robert Lanza extends this into a newer theory called biocentrism. In his book, *Biocentrism: How Life and Consciousness are the Keys to Understanding the Nature of the Universe*, Lanza claims that life doesn't end as the physical body dies. He claims the theory of biocentrism teaches that death as we know it is an illusion and that our consciousness creates the universe, and not the other way round.

According to biocentrism, space and time are not the hard objects we think they are. Wave your hand through the air—what do you see? Nothing. Look in the mirror at your head. Do you see the thoughts and formations surrounding your brain? According to Lanza, space and time are simply the tools for putting everything together, and so death does not exist in a timeless, spaceless world.

This isn't much different than what Albert Einstein, one of the world's most influential physicists, taught when he said, "A human being is a part of the whole called by us universe, a part limited in time and space. He experiences himself, his thoughts and feelings as something separated from the rest, a kind of optical delusion of his consciousness. This delusion is a kind of prison for us, restricting us to our personal desires and to affection for a few persons nearest to us. Our task must be to free ourselves from this prison by widening our circle of compassion to embrace all living creatures and the whole of nature in its beauty."

When an old friend of Einstein passed, he wrote, "Now Besso has departed from this strange world a little ahead of me. That means nothing. People like us ... know that the distinction between past, present, and future is only a stubbornly persistent illusion."

Ralph Waldo Emerson, American essayist, lecturer, and poet, who led the Transcendentalist movement, said, "The influences of the senses has in most men overpowered the mind to the degree that the walls of space and time have come to look real and insurmountable; and to speak with levity of these limits is, in the world, the sign of insanity."

Have we convinced ourselves that dead is dead? Have we convinced ourselves that our loved ones are locked up, unable to be with us, in some sort of sadistic punishment for both them and us, as a means to help or hurt us?

Chapter Three

Signs from the Other Side

You don't need a medium to figure out your connections; you just need to connect the dots. If you smell a man's cologne, is it the same as your father's or grandfather's? If you are receiving coins in random places, it is probably a sign from a loved one. Or a bird that sits on your windowsill who won't leave is more than likely a sign from a loved one on the Other Side who wants you to see the beauty around you. Or maybe you are seeing a repetitive pattern of numbers such as 111 or 222, etc.—this isn't coincidental, but a sign from the Other Side for you. Once you pay attention, ground yourself, and awaken all of your senses—most of all your sixth sense—you will find that it is more than likely Mom, Dad, Grandma, Grandpa, etc., just wanting you to be aware of the Afterlife. After all, it isn't called the afterdead, is it?

Hello from Heaven

Can our loved ones in Heaven really communicate with us? Absolutely! Loved ones on the Other Side want to communicate with you as much as you want to talk to them. Just as if a relative moves across the country and you have to learn how to communicate differently, the same is true with those who've crossed. As I mentioned earlier, those on the Other Side don't have vocal cords, so they try to get through in the loudest way possible, but sometimes that isn't even loud, or many consider the signs pure coincidences. Have you ever been sitting down, deep in thought, and your spouse or kids finally got your attention after telling you they tried several times over? Think how frustrating it must be for your loved ones to try to get your attention when they aren't here in the physical. Paying attention to the various signs and symbols may help you recognize that you have been getting those hellos from Heaven!

Probably one of the most common questions that I receive during medium sessions is, "Are they okay?" followed by, "Do they know how much I miss/love them?" If you watch any of the television shows that have mediums on them, the shared main message is, "He/She loves you and is doing fine." Although in each of their cases it might seem they are doing fine, it might not *always* be the case. It doesn't mean that a loved one is sitting in a fiery pit of scorching hot fire (I will talk about this later on), but our loved ones worry about us on the Other Side just as much we do them. They do better when we do better. And they can help us when we allow them to.

Free Will: Free Choice

His friends and family called him Mack. He was about 6'5",
in his late twenties, and had dark black hair, cut short. I didn't
need any psychic abilities to sense his nervousness.

"I'm Kristy," I introduced myself with a friendly smile. I
pointed to the chair across from mine, moving the white table
that sat between the seats to give him some more leg room.

Mack took a seat and looked around at my brightcolored
office adorned with comfortable furniture, plush pillows, positive quotes on the walls, and shelves and shelves of owls, all
gifts from clients from around the world. "This isn't what I expected," he noted, still taking in everything in my small office.

I laughed in response. I get that a lot, especially from men.
"What did you expect, black walls, cut-up chickens, and crystal balls?" I joked.

Mack laughed a throaty laugh and shook his head. "Stupid, I know. I guess I didn't know what to expect," he admitted.

The laughter thankfully broke some of his tension and I
began to explain my process of reading. "I connect with your
energy and call on your guides, angels, and your loved ones on
the Other Side along with my guides, angels, and loved ones,
too, because sometimes they can help make the connection
clearer. Our guides and loved ones help us along our life journey, but they can't make us do anything different. We all have
free will and free choice; they just see a wider perspective—a
panoramic vision instead of the tunnel vision that we often
use instead."

Mack nodded, but I knew he didn't understand, and to be honest, I think he just wanted it to be over with.

"I see your loved ones just like I see you. But conversation for me isn't quite as fluid as you and me talking. It is more like charades with them. So if someone's name is Teddy, they may show me a teddy bear. And it doesn't always make sense right now, but take the information, because as much as I try not to be cryptic or confusing, I don't always connect the dots. It isn't my job to analyze, but to be the messenger. So, let's begin, shall we?"

I closed my eyes and had Mack tell me his full name out loud. It was my way of dialing his loved one's phone numbers and calling them forward. As soon as I closed my eyes, I could sense two energies walking forward and when I opened my eyes, I saw that the first man looked like an older version of Mack and the other was a male similarly aged to Mack, but was shorter and thinner.

The older man showed me that he was Mack's dad and said that the male next to him was Mack's brother. Mack's dad showed me a car accident with him driving.

"Mack, your dad and brother are here, standing next to you, actually. He said that he, you, your brother, and your mom were all in the car at the same time when the accident happened. He shows me alcohol, but says it was the other driver who hit you."

I could hear Mack's sobs, but I didn't want to stop because I didn't want to interrupt Mack's dad.

"He says you were sitting behind your mom, in back of the passenger seat."

Mack nodded and took a deep breath that started the sobs again.

"You weren't supposed to die, Mack." I repeated what his dad told me. "You asked to drive, he said, and he told you no and you were mad. Now he says you are still mad."

Mack looked up at me with his water-filled Irish green eyes. "I'm not mad at him. I think he's mad at me. Is he mad at me, Kristy? Is my brother mad at me? I should've died. I should've been the one driving. I took his spot in the car and in Heaven!"

I looked over at Mack's dad and his brother. They both shook their heads no at me. A deep feeling of sorrow emitted from all three of them. Nobody was mad at anybody; it was just an unfortunate situation for everyone involved.

"They are absolutely not mad at you, Mack. They are upset at what happened, but they aren't angry with you. Your dad feels as if they were stolen, but that doesn't mean they shifted the destiny of your death." Mack's dad interjected with a fatherly lecture for me to pass along. "They want you to go on with your life. They say this happened about five years ago and you've stopped living, which has made both of them stop living."

Mack gave me a confused look.

"We live in Heaven. We live in the Afterlife. Your dad says his favorite thing to do is fish and that he lives on a small lake. Your brother, he loves sports, especially baseball, and he helps kids who pass because of unfortunate accidents, and he plays games with them. They also watch over you and your mom, along with your son—the son you named after your dad."

Mack shook his head. "How did you know?"

"I don't know, they do." I smiled, pointing to his dad and brother standing in spirit. "And you can be a better man and a better dad than what you've allowed yourself to be."

Mack's eyes went blank for a moment. "Are they okay, Kristy?"

"They will be better if you are okay. Your dad says your mom has found a nice partner and he approves of him."

"He does?" Mack scoffed, surprised.

I nodded. Not everyone on the Other Side approves of their love's new partners so it's always interesting to hear their opinions. "Yes, he says that he treats her well and that although he isn't him, she deserves to be happy, and you should be too," I added. "She isn't crossing over anytime soon. She deserves to be happy just like you do. And just a side note, your dad says he's better looking than your mom's significant other."

Mack clapped his hands together and let out a yelp. "Dad would say that too," he grinned. "And it is true!"

Mack's dad grew serious: *Tell him that our conscious will be clearer when he clears his own. We will live when he lives. We stop living when he stops living.*

I passed along the message and allowed Mack to let the messages settle in.

"Can I give you a hug?" Mack asked me as I showed him to the door.

"Of course," I said as Mack laid his head on my shoulder and cried for a few more minutes as I held him. It was like a dishrag being wrung out. It wasn't just his grief, it was as if Mack's soul was being washed clean to start again.

"Can I see you again?" Mack asked, as he wiped his eyes with the back of his t-shirt.

"Yes, but I don't think you'll need to, Mack. Just spend some time getting to know how to communicate with your dad and brother on the Other Side. They will show you the signs when they are around."

He stepped out of the office, into the hallway, and turned around quickly. "Kristy, is my son my brother or my dad?"

"Do you mean have either of them reincarnated?" I shook my head no. "Nope, but that boy was chosen by them for you. Enjoy him. And take him fishing when he gets older," I voiced. "Oh, and next year there will be a new baby girl."

I never saw Mack again, but his mom came to see me a little over a year after his appointment with a new wedding ring on her finger, which Mack's dad was happy about, and pictures of both of her grandchildren—her husband's namesake and a new baby girl.

We Are Who We Are

I wish I could say that once the shell of our bodies die we sprout wings and set down all of our earthly burdens and troubles, but we don't. We don't change our personalities or lose the memories of our earthly journey when we make our Afterlife trip. All of that is instilled within our soul and our spirit. So if someone was ornery in this lifetime, they will be the same on the Other Side, unless they work on it there. If someone was bitter over this or that, they will continue to be bitter and resentful unless they do the soul work to release it.

So are they all okay when they cross over? The answer is actually pretty simple. They can be okay if they allow themselves to be okay. The free will and free choice we have in this existence is the same we have when we die. We have free will and free choice to cross into the light. And we have free will and free choice to allow our Heaven to be the best Heaven possible.

On a daily basis, in my office, on social media, and through e-mail and messages I witness the struggle that people go through and how it encompasses all parts of life, with a direct domino effect. Struggle is nothing new, but when it is us going through it, we forget that others are going through it too. The loneliness and the black clouds shadow any sunshine, and for many, any positivity even feels like poison. Yet without any action, those struggling begin to feel as if they are drowning a slow death.

Just as we are taught not to panic in the water, finding calmness within the storm of struggle has to be a priority. Or as philosopher and revolutionary socialist Rosa Luxemburg is quoted as saying, "Those who do not move, do not notice their chains." And those same chains can bind us when we cross. If we don't feel deserving of Heaven, then we disallow ourselves from having a wonderful Afterlife. Some believe that is called Hell. Not necessarily the fire-and-brimstone kind, but maybe even worse, a personal hell of feeling not good enough or worthy enough, for eternity.

New Beginnings

Lizzie was a petite twenty-something brunette who came to see me for a psychic session, not mediumship. "I don't really have anybody that I need to connect with," she murmured. The interesting thing was that there was a gentleman standing next to her. He was wearing a brown suit and a hat.

"What if I don't know what I want to do with my life?" she asked, her emerald green eyes welling up.

"It's not imperative to know the exact path of your life, step-by-step," I challenged her. "I realize that seems ironic for a psychic to say, but I have found that being comfortable with yourself, in your own shoes, will bring the most joy. And if you can do that, the passion will meet you along the way. Just be careful of people who will try to control that joy, happiness, and passion. Even those who claim they love and support you."

Lizzie slowly nodded.

I could sense something else was going on, so I continued. "It's a boy, though, right? He hurts you ... !"

"No!" Lizzie defended.

I gave her my "I'm a psychic" look and she nodded and began to cry.

She grabbed a tissue from my blue end table, blew her nose, and then got up out of her chair. Facing a sign on my wall that read "Believe," she confessed to me about all of the abuse.

The drinking. The drinking and driving. The drugs. And the physical and emotional abuse.

"Let me help you, Lizzie. I've been there. Let me help you," I repeated. "You have the opportunity to take back control of your life. Your grandpa shows me how much you always wanted to be a nurse."

"My who?" she asked me, confused, still staring at the wall.

"There is a grandfather here who says you never knew him. He's your dad's dad. He says that you can go back to school and become a nurse—even with the baby," I quietly added.

Lizzie swung quickly around, looked at me, and put her hand on her belly. The tears began again. "I never knew my grandpa. He died before I was born. He's here?"

"He is. It doesn't matter if you met him or not, he is connected to you. You even have his nose," I laughed. "Do you want to know what sex the baby is?" I smiled, trying to lighten the intense mood.

"I think it's a girl," she confessed. "Nobody knows that I'm pregnant, Kristy—not my boyfriend, my family… nobody."

"It is a girl," I confirmed. I thought for a moment before continuing. I saw a pile of white feathers; ever since I was a child white feathers were a sign for me that a death would occur. It made me worry that she might miscarry, so I pushed the vision away. "If your daughter was standing in front of you in the same situation, what would you say to her, Liz?"

She sat back down on the chair across from me and quickly responded with more tears pouring down her face. "I'd tell her to leave the loser and that I would help her go back to school."

During the remainder of the hour we came up with a plan. It wasn't just about exiting her relationship, or how to handle being a single mom, it was much more than that. It was creating her destiny. As we talked she realized that she had abandoned the people who had never once left her side, even on the darkest days. She realized that she had stopped singing. She realized that she wasn't even dreaming at night. Nor was she dreaming in the daytime. Goals change and evolve and are sometimes shelved, but they can always be brought back to life. Lizzie left my office with a plan.

The news article in the local paper the next day was brief, but words didn't have to be spelled out in order to be fully understood.

A one-car rollover accident occurred in the late hours, killing the passenger. The driver was taken to an area hospital, but released with only minor injuries. A preliminary investigation says that alcohol was a factor in the crash.

What the readers wouldn't know was that it wasn't one who died in that accident, but two—Lizzie and her baby.

It took me a long time to stop blaming myself. Even though it was up to Lizzie to not get into that car, I felt guilty, but it was her own choice. If a doctor hands you a prescription to take, he doesn't walk you to the pharmacy, and he doesn't stand over you every single day watching you take the pill—it is up to you. The same goes with your life. Destiny is a choice, and there are many paths that can be taken. It doesn't mean that every bad choice will result in bad things (or loss of life), but I do know that how you handle your choices, and your reactions, sets a precedence for your future, here and in the Afterlife.

I told Lizzie that I didn't believe she needed to plan her life out, step-by-step, and I still believe that advice. But in her honor (and in her unborn child's honor), I would like to share with you some words of wisdom that may help you, or someone you know, reclaim a destiny.

1. Release the grudges. Whether they are toward yourself or someone else.

2. Stop beating yourself up for your mistakes.

3. Learn to trust yourself.

4. Be careful of making decisions based purely off of emotions.

5. Be gentle with yourself—make sure that your expectations aren't too high and too costly.

6. Talk to someone you trust.

7. Make sure there is something that you are focusing on.

8. Make sure you are focused on the right now and not the past.

9. Give yourself time—change won't
   happen overnight. Small improvements
   make huge strides in the long run.

10. Spend time with quality people and
    not because you feel bad for them.

A philosopher once said that "every new beginning comes from some other beginning's end." Unfortunately, Lizzie's new beginning comes on the Other Side. And yet other peoples' new beginnings are divorce, or unemployment, or a lawsuit, or death of a loved one. There is constant loss around us each day, but it is up to us to see the new beginnings and to create our destiny. Allow that destiny to evolve but take control of it.

By working on things in your lifetime and clearing your conscious—work that Mack had to do and Lizzie had to do on the Other Side—you don't have to work so hard when you cross into the Afterlife. Think of it as getting all of your work done before heading off to vacation. You don't want to come back from vacation with a pile on your desk; you want to enjoy your time without that hanging over your head. The same is for true for life, death, and Afterlife.

It takes practice to gain confidence and to make the connection with your loved ones who have passed, because oftentimes when the connection is made it is thought to be the result of an overactive imagination, or the belief that you are only receiving what you are trying to receive. We come to believe that what we're receiving isn't true and real, so we just hang up the phone and break communication.

Just like when you take a test and the first answer you think of is often the right one, the first thought is often the intuitive information. After that, your logical mind takes over and creates doubt. The more you continue to dial the phone, the easier it will be to make that connection to the Other Side.

Chapter Four

Objects and Trinkets

The Other Side loves to leave trinkets and coins for you to find to remind you that your loved ones are still around. Items are often placed in our path to give us that Heaven hello. The list is endless as to what might be sent to us, but the most common items seem to include coins and feathers.

Even though the item you find may seem random, there is normally a reason behind it; you just have to spend some time and energy to jog your memory. If you find a coin in your path look at its year to see if perhaps there is significance between you and your loved one. It might be an anniversary year, a birth year, or even a passing year. If you find a cross, it could be from a family member who was religious.

The White Feathers

The call was something she never imagined. It couldn't be possible. No, it wasn't possible. She stared at her cell phone, not sure what to do, or who to call.

Jackie always believed her dad to be invincible. Always in good health, she couldn't remember him being sick even one time in her thirty-something years. He was still working full-time, so how? It didn't make sense. Jackie plopped herself onto a dining room chair.

"Dad." She put her head on the table and started to cry. "How could you leave without a goodbye?"

"Jack … ?"

She lifted her head and saw her husband standing in the doorway holding their one-year-old daughter, Russia, in his arms.

"My mom just called. My dad was on his way to lunch and he had a medical emergency"—Jackie stopped for a moment, not believing the words that she was saying—"and ran his car into a tree."

Jackie's husband, Matthew, set Russia down on the floor and walked over to Jackie and wrapped his arms around her in a hug. "He's okay, though, right?" Matthew never had a father figure in his life and Walt was like his own father. They were friends and fishing buddies.

Jackie shook her head and started gasping back tears. Matthew stared, waiting for the punch line to a joke. Walt was probably so angry about messing up his car, Matthew thought. But Jackie's gasps turned to sobs and hysterical crying and he realized that there was no joke; Walt was dead.

Matthew leaned over to pick up Russia when he noticed something in her hands. "What's that you have, Rush?" He pulled the long, white object out of her pudgy fingers; it was a feather. "How did you get this?" he asked, confused for a moment, and then he looked at Jackie, who had calmed down for a moment.

Jackie took the white feather from Matthew and gently cradled it. "It's from Dad. It has to be from Dad!"

Matthew didn't argue and held his baby girl and his beloved wife in his arms.

The funeral was unbearable. This was the first person Jackie had ever lost and she knew that she was lucky. Both sets of grandparents were alive, and to see the look on her dad's mom's face was heart shattering.

An aneurysm, the coroner had determined, had taken Walt's life. Everybody was just so thankful that during lunch hour traffic, Walt didn't hit or injure anybody. It was just like him, too, friends and family members at the funeral continually said. He was the kind of man who would pull over to the side of the freeway to help change a stranger's tire. Or give a few dollars to the homeless man on the corner. It would have mortified him in life and in death if anybody else had gotten hurt because of him. He was probably upset about the tree that he hit, Jackie teased affectionately to her husband during the showing. That was just the kind of person her father was.

As the casket was being lowered into the grave, the minister read from the script. "He will cover you with his feathers. He will shelter you with his wings. His faithful promises are your armor and protection. Psalm 91:4." Jackie hung her head down in prayer. When she opened her eyes, she saw a feather laying on the ground in front of her. She bent over and picked it up. Smiling, she silently showed Matthew.

It was several years later when her daughter Russia was taken to the hospital for stomach pains. Her appendix needed to be removed as soon as possible. Although a routine surgery, Russia's blood count was disturbing to the surgeon, and the doctor confessed that she was concerned that Russia might have leukemia.

Jackie and Matthew sat in the hospital waiting room. The fluorescent lights couldn't even brighten up the darkness and worry that enveloped them. Jackie bent down and began to pray and then asked her dad to be there, to help. She opened her eyes and was stunned at what she saw. A large feather laid in front her, as if it fell out of nowhere. Before she could point it out to Matthew, the surgeon came over to give the good news—it was just appendicitis and Russia was okay.

Jackie's tears began to flow, but this time they were tears of relief. "Thanks, Dad," she said, holding the feather close to her chest.

On Earth he was always dependable and prompt, and on the Other Side he was the same. Feathers continued to appear in unexpected places, always at the times when Jackie was missing her dad or needed him the most. And on her fireplace mantel, next to a picture of her father, is a jar of feathers from Heaven.

Treasure the Treasures

Whenever I conduct a séance or a gallery reading, I honestly never know what to expect, so I expect the unexpected, and it seems that our loved ones on the Other Side like that best anyhow. (One particular March's séance was no different.) As three participants sat down at the table, I closed my eyes and called on their loved ones to come forward to give me messages to pass along. One lovely lady in spirit stood next to the participant to my right, Kara. The woman in spirit smiled at me and then asked me to inquire where the teacups were.

"Kara, do you have your grandmother's or great-grandmother's teacups or china?"

"Uhhh…I think I do."

"Buried? In a closet, put away?"

"Probably," she replied giving me a strange look.

"I am supposed to tell you that they were her treasures, and they should be yours too. Take them out and use them, don't store them away."

Make my treasures, your treasures.

Kara dug out the china that weekend and made what I can only imagine was a delicious meal and served it on the vintage pink-flowered Syracuse Federal China. And as her grandma stated, can you imagine all of the celebrations those dishes had witnessed? But why wait for a celebration? So she made grilled pork tenderloin, boiled fingerling potatoes with garlic, and steamed broccoli.

It's so often that we bury our treasures, whether they are the words of love, or treasures like Kara's dishes. We get so hung up on housework, complaining about weather, yelling at or about our kids, spouses, bosses, coworkers, etc., that what really matters is the last thing that we do or we say. But maybe it is time to get our priorities in order. The priorities, or the treasures, that truly matter.

Found Keys

Years ago I had a client named Amie who lost her husband to a quick-moving cancer. She kept asking him for a sign, but it wasn't until six months to the date of his passing when she woke up one morning and grabbed her glasses off her nightstand only to find a key sitting there. She knew the key wasn't there when she went to bed, and she had absolutely no clue where it came from. After that, it became almost a daily occurrence for her to find keys—in the bottom of her purse, on the kitchen counter, in parking lots, on her desk at work. No matter where she went, she kept finding keys.

"They are the keys to nothing and nowhere, Kristy," she complained to me during the session. "I'm not even sure they are from Dale. Why couldn't I have a butterfly or something a bit more self-explanatory?"

Dale stood in front of me shaking a large ring of keys, dropping them and then picking them up. He smiled mischievously at me, urging me to mention it.

"Did he work maintenance or with cars?" I asked. "Where he would've had to use a lot of keys?"

"Nope, he had a desk job and worked on a computer," Amie responded.

I looked back at Dale who shook his head and again jingled the ring of keys, dropped them, and picked them back up. Then I heard him say to mention when they first met.

"He said to think back to when you first met…"

Before I could get the rest of the sentence out, Amie's eyes grew large and the tears began to fall.

"Dale and I met at a gas station," Aimie began, taking a tissue and wiping her face. "I was in a hurry and ran in to pay for my gas and to get a pop. There was this very handsome man with a big smile and I accidently bumped into him and made him drop his fountain pop and his keys. He should've been rude to me; it was a mess. Instead of yelling, he asked me for my phone number, and a year later we were married. I forgot all about that."

"So do you want a butterfly instead?" I teased.

Aimee laughed. "Nope, the keys make much more sense. But what does he think about hundred dollar bills?"

Aleve

Lou's only brother and best friend Ronnie passed away unexpectedly after a freak house fire claimed his life. He smelled smoke in the garage and tried fervently to put out the fire, fearful of an explosion from the the lawn mower and several cans of gasoline that sat nearby. In his panic, his clothes caught on fire and he was burned over 70 percent of his body. Infection quickly spread and he passed away only a few days later.

Before Ronnie's passing, he would take a form of pain reliever called Aleve to help with his aches and pains from arthritis. It was the day of his memorial and Lou pulled her outfit out of the closet, along with her dress shoes that she hadn't worn for quite some time. As she stepped into the shoe she felt what she assumed was a small pebble. She slid the shoe off her foot, turned it upside down, and out fell an Aleve.

"I don't have any Aleve in my house. I've never bought that brand and I've never taken one," Lou said, still surprised by the sign even though it had been almost ten years ago. "Every so often, and it seems that it happens when I am missing him the most, I find a random Aleve in the hallway or just sitting on the counter. I live by myself, so I know that it's Ronnie popping in to say hello. There isn't any other explanation."

Rocks

Michael passed just a week after his sixteenth birthday. He had gone out with friends to the lake and had accidently drowned. Michael always loved nature and even as a little boy would pick up rocks. His mom, Shannon, was always dumping various rocks out of his pants and into a mason jar that she kept in the laundry room.

"I don't know how our washer survived as many years as it did because there were many times I would miss some," Shannon shared. "Michael particularly liked heart-shaped rocks. Even though he was a boy, he was sensitive and had a huge heart himself." She sniffled and pulled out a large heart-shaped rock from her purse, and then a smaller one and another and another until she had over twenty rocks sitting on the white table that sat between her chair and mine.

"This was from Michael's collection?" I asked in awe, picking up the largest stone. It wasn't that the rocks sort of resembled hearts, it was almost as if they were carved.

"No, these are all the stones I've found since he passed six months ago. I found the one you're holding at the cemetery the day he was buried. I just looked down and there it was."

"How comforting for you," I remarked, still amazed.

"I don't even look for them, they just seem to be right where I am when I need a sign the most. I just look down and there one is."

Shannon was obviously still hurting and the rocks didn't necessarily heal her wounds, but they reassured her that although Michael was not physically there, he was still there in the only way that he could be, communicating the only way that he could. I was most impressed by Shannon's recognition of her sign, especially so soon after her son's passing.

Grief has a way of creating a veil around us so that if the sign were a hippo and that hippo came strolling in wearing a pink tutu and did a dance in front of us, rarely would we notice.

So if you have just recently lost someone and haven't received a sign and are frustrated and left wondering, don't fret. Instead, ask your loved ones for a sign and be clear and concise as to what you want it to be. Just as Shannon doesn't scour fields looking for a heart-shaped rock, you, too, should just let the signs naturally happen. We all seem to want to control everything and the Other Side is something as far from controllable as you can get. Just because you aren't seeing anything doesn't mean that it isn't there.

Coins

There are many myths within different cultures referring to coins and the dead. In Greek mythology, Charon, the ferryman of Hades, required payment for his services when someone passed away. And so to make certain that a loved one was given a ride across the rivers Styx and Acheron and into an everlasting world, a coin was placed in the mouth of the departed so that they weren't left to wander the shore for eternity.

In England and in the United States, pennies were placed on the closed eyes of the dead. Although exactly why is not known, it is theorized that it was either to make sure that the eyes of the departed didn't open during the funeral or to alert someone that the person wasn't truly dead.

Today, many mementos, including coins, are left on tombstones and graves.

Coins are one way that those we love on the Other Side get our attention and show us they are around. There are thousands of stories from people who soon after losing a loved one began finding coins in random places. The most common coins people say they find are pennies and dimes.

Some people understand what the sign means when they receive the coin from their loved one. It could be that their loved one collected coins or that change was important for something like lunch money or a special vacation they saved up for. But not all have significance and just helps to get attention.

Dimes

Brandy had been doing ballroom dance since she was five years old. As she was a spirited little girl, the sport offered her the ability to channel her energy. It wasn't long before everyone—her parents, grandparents, and coaches—knew that Brandy was destined for great things in dance.

Brandy's grandma, her dad's mom, was her caregiver after school while both of her parents worked full-time jobs. Grandma Gabrielle, or Gadgy, as Brandy called her, was really more like a mom than a grandma. She went over Brandy's homework, disciplined her, took her to and from her dance classes, taught Brandy how to cook, sew, and knit. Gadgy's husband, Allen, had passed away before Brandy was born and although Brandy's mom often told stories of her dad, Brandy loved Gadgy's stories from when they were courting.

Gadgy also loved to ballroom dance, but Allen wasn't as in love with it as she was. He was, however, in love with his wife. Gadgy would say that every day when she got up, he would tell her that on a scale of one to ten, she was his ten. In today's world some may see that as insulting and demeaning, but it made Gadgy feel loved and pretty. She would sweetly swat Allen's shoulder and blush.

Every Friday evening, Gadgy and Allen would go to their ballroom dance class and then out to dinner. As much as Allen complained, he loved spending time with his wife. He was made fun of by the guys at work for his seemingly forced extracurricular activity, but he would just tell them they were jealous. He had a ten for a wife and they didn't.

Brandy grew up in a small town in Oklahoma. The same town that her mom and dad grew up in. The same town that both of her grandparents grew up in. Everybody loved Allen. He was outgoing and loved to chit-chat with everyone, including strangers. It was his always-helpful personality that was the reason he died.

It was a summer afternoon and Allen had stopped in at the local diner to get a cup of coffee before he headed home. He had worked at the electric company since he was just sixteen years old, but the last few months had been exceptionally stressful. The economy had taken a dive and his bosses were incredibly moody, which in turn resulted in the workers being dumped on.

For the most part, Allen brushed their rants off, but that day it was extremely warm and the storm outside that was churning was also churning inside of him. After about the hundredth unfair critique, Allen threw his work shirt down, yelled that he was taking the rest of the day off on personal time and punched out. He was fairly certain that he wouldn't be fired, but after forty years of employment there, he was tired.

It certainly wasn't the way it had been when he first started. Then, everybody had taken care of one another and had cared for one another. Now he was just a number and it frustrated him because he knew that it wouldn't change. And he figured that when he went in the next day he would be written up. Yeah, he could have a bit of a mouth on him, he thought, but there were times you could only take so much. It was a good thing he didn't drink like his Pap, he laughed. He would be drunk today for sure! Coffee was his strongest drink.

"Anything else I can get you, Allen?" Earl, the owner of the coffee shop asked him, filling up Allen's coffee cup.

Allen dumped two creams, ripped open two sugars, and swirled it with his spoon. "Nah." He shook his head. "Gab has probably already heard about my tantrum. I should probably go home."

Allen took a swig of his coffee and placed two dollars and five dimes on the light blue Formica table.

"I don't know how you constantly have a supply of dimes," Earl chuckled as he scooped up the money and placed it in his apron pocket.

Allen shrugged. "I like the number ten. I married a ten. My daughter is a ten and, well, dimes represent my life—a perfect ten."

Earl shook his head and added, "Except for today, right? What is today?"

Allen joined in on the laugh, but didn't add anything; he just exited and waved goodbye. As he walked to his car he fumbled for his keys out of his jeans pocket, dropping a dime on the ground. He bent over to pick it up, and just as he stood upright he saw a man, wearing a black jacket and black jeans, on the other side of his car. Noticing the man's unusual attire for the sweltering heat, Allen realized that the man was trying to break into his car. Instead of confronting the man, Allen tried to start a conversation.

"Can I help ya?" Allen asked in a friendly tone.

The man just stood there, staring at Allen. Allen reached into his pocket and pulled out a twenty-dollar bill. "Here, take this. It should get you a bus ticket."

The man didn't reply; he just slowly walked toward Allen, but before Allen realized it, the stranger took a crowbar that he held in his right hand and lunged at Allen, hitting him over the head. He grabbed the keys, the twenty-dollar bill, and took off.

It was the squeal of the tires that made Earl look out the window to see Allen lying on the asphalt parking lot and Allen's car speeding down the road toward the freeway. He yelled for his cook to call 911 and Allen's wife, then Earl raced out the door to assist.

"After three days the doctors told me that I needed to make a decision," Gadgy told Brandy. It was a story that Brandy often asked to hear, and although painful, her grandma recognized that it was the good and the bad stories that helped to keep her grandpa's spirit alive for her.

"And then you found the dime?" Brandy asked.

Gadgy nodded. "I was contemplating what to do. It isn't an easy decision to take someone off of life support. You pray that there will be a miracle, even if the doctors tell you that it is unlikely. Your mom stayed with your grandpa while I walked to the hospital chapel. I sat down in the pew and began to cry, as I am sure most people do in hospital chapels. But it was only a few minutes after I sat down when I felt pressure on my shoulder, as if someone was touching me. I thought maybe it was your mom or one of the doctors, so I opened my eyes and turned around, but nobody was there. I bent my head again to say a prayer when I noticed the shiny dime lying on the chapel floor. I picked it up and knew it was the spirit of your grandpa and that the dime was a sign that I had to do what I had to do."

"How did you know that it wasn't a sign that he would wake up?"

Gadgy bit her bottom lip and closed her eyes for a moment, thinking back to the day she lost her best friend. It was a question she had asked herself for fourteen years. "It was just something that I felt. He would never have wanted me to keep him on those machines. He was too much of a firecracker to lay in bed, or a wheelchair if he did awaken. After all of the machines were disconnected, I held his hand and he peacefully passed away." Gadgy teared up.

"And then I came along!" Brandy exclaimed.

"It was the day of Grandpa Allen's funeral when your mom took the pregnancy test. We were happy, but sad because we knew he would've been so excited. He would've been a wonderful grandpa."

Although Gadgy had told the story numerous times, it didn't stop affecting her. What she told Brandy was the truth.

Allen would've been a very hands-on grandpa just like he was a hands-on dad to their only daughter. "I always felt that you and your grandpa met in Heaven and he is the one who gifted you the love of dance as a way to make us all happy."

"I'm nervous about this weekend's competition, Gadgy," Brandy confessed. "Now that I'm in my teens, I can't win over the judges with my cuteness anymore," she playfully teased.

Gadgy laughed. Even some of the outrageous things that Brandy came up with sounded like her Allen.

"You've got this, Brandy," Gadgy reassured her, getting up to put the potatoes on to boil. "Well, look there." She pointed to the ground where a shiny dime lay. "I think your grandpa agrees. You are a ten just like your good ole Gadgy."

Brandy picked up the dime and smiled. "You still find these often, don't you?"

Gadgy nodded and smiled. "It seems whenever I need a pick-me-up I find the dimes. Sometimes it seems as if they come from thin air, but I know exactly who they come from."

The dance competition was the next day. Gadgy had sewn both Brandy's and her partner's costume. As Gadgy sat in her sewing room making some final adjustments, her thoughts drifted back to the conversation about Allen. She sure missed him. She looked over at the mason jars that she had filled up with the dimes she'd found. Every year she would take the money she collected and donate it to a charity that dealt with brain injuries. Allen would've wanted that.

Even though she believed in Heaven and she was glad that she received her signs, she was still lonely. She masked her sadness with strength and with Brandy and all of her activities. She had done that for almost fifteen years and she knew that soon enough Brandy would be off to college and on to her own life. "And then what?" She spoke it out loud, as if expecting a response, and laughed when all she heard was her cat meow at her. *Probably wondering what is wrong with the crazy lady*, she said to herself.

She got up from the sewing table, stretched, turned off the lights, and walked into her bedroom. She grabbed the television remote, turned on the television, and began to undress when the shiny silver object caught her attention. It was smack dab in the middle of the bed—a dime. She just shook her head in disbelief, took the dime, walked back to the sewing room, and tossed it into her mason jar. "Dollar bills, Allen, what about dollar bills," she murmured.

The next day, she met Brandy, her daughter, and son-in-law at the dance hall for the competition.

Brandy changed into her costume and looked in the mirror. Normally not nervous, she couldn't shake the tension she felt. She took a deep breath, grabbed the lipstick off of the vanity, and right next to the makeup case was a shiny dime, face up. It was almost as if she could hear her grandpa, the one she had never met on the earthly plane, say, "No matter what, you will always be a ten."

Brandy and her partner came in third place in the competition, but no matter, it didn't dull Brandy's mood. After she told everyone her find in the dressing room, her Gadgy smiled and silently thanked Allen. It would have been just like him to be that supporter in life and in death.

"You are my ten, Allen. Forever and ever," Gadgy whispered.

Gadgy continued to find dimes, as did her daughter and her granddaughter Brandy.

Call Me

Jeff, a middle-aged man, came in for a life coaching session, and I immediately connected with his mom on the Other Side.

"She keeps showing me dimes, Jeff," I said. "What is the significance with dimes or with the number ten?" I asked him.

Jeff laughed in disbelief; he had come in for help with finding his life purpose and for me to go over his resume, and didn't think his session would go quite like it was going. "I have actually seen dimes flip out of thin air and land on the floor right in front of me—most of the time when I am thinking or talking about Mom. I rarely talk about this except to my family," he explained. "I'm so worried someone will think I am nuts!"

I smiled as his mom showed me several Ziploc bags filled with coins. "She shows me a whole lot of coins!"

"I keep all my coins, and have a quart-size bag filled with about four pounds or more," Jeff validated.

"Is there a meaning with dimes?" I asked.

"My grandfather passed away in 1988, when I was just nine years old. He worked for the telephone company collecting the change from payphones. Back then you would use dimes to make a call," he said, shaking his head at how many changes in life have occurred. "Well, at his funeral the officiating minister joked and told us that dimes would more than likely be significant in letting our family know he was with us and that to call on him when we need him. It was that very day, on the way to the funeral luncheon when we found our first dime right there in the parking lot. My entire family continues to find dimes in the most unusual spots. I don't know if the officiate was being insightful or just playing with us, but the 'dime find,' as we call it, is a comforting sign and reassures us that grandpa is our guardian angel."

The Meaning

In numerology the dime, being a ten-cent piece, would be $1+0=1$. One refers to the beginning and is a perfect number. Perfect numbers in numerology show balance, the good and the bad, the positive and the negative, the Yin and the Yang. Some people view finding a dime to represent their loved ones telling them that through all of the bad (the death), that they have found good (the Other Side). The number ten also means coming full circle and beginning again. Ten also represents fulfillment, attainment, and completion, and so it is believed that symbolic dimes provide the messages of lost opportunities that are now regained. The penny, being a one-cent piece, has a similar message of new beginnings.

Pennies from Heaven

The morning was cool and it felt great to throw on a sweatshirt as I left the house for my daily jog. I couldn't find my headphones and was mildly irritated; I needed the motivation of listening to Blaine and Allyson of 96.3 in Detroit and their banter to get my jog on, and without that I thought I would just take a quick brisk walk.

Even though it was a Tuesday, all was quiet in the neighborhood with just a passing jogger here and there with whom I would exchange a silent smile or a wave. As I rounded the park near my home, I got a terrible cramp in my leg and began to panic—I had left my phone at home since I couldn't find my headphones. What if I couldn't get home?

I leaned up against a large oak tree, and I noticed movement on the metal park bench. An elderly man with mussed-up gray hair sat there wearing a crisp white dress shirt, dark gray slacks, and he had a suit jacket lying across his lap. Next to him sat a beautiful woman with a pink scarf wrapped around her head, a light blue sweatshirt with *Grandma* stitched on it, and she was wearing blue jeans. But this man wasn't looking at her—he just stared forward and sobbed.

"Peg, how could you? How could you leave me?" he wailed.

Tears immediately streamed down my face as I realized that he was dressed for Peg's funeral.

The woman with the pink scarf sat there in spirit with her hand on her husband's left leg. I could tell by her aura that she hadn't crossed over yet. Her energy ached with sadness, yet she was relieved of the physical pain she had endured for so long.

"You said you would live, Peg. You said you would make it," he continued, anger and sadness pouring out with each word. "Do you hear me? Do you even hear me?"

The lady looked over at me, knowing that I could see her, and I felt stuck. But the elderly man was in such distress I feared he was going to do something drastic that would keep them apart for some time. And so I quietly made my way to the park bench, limping, and trying to ignore the pain in my leg that nowhere matched the pain that Peg's husband felt in his heart and soul.

In my head I asked Peg what her husband's name was. I've always been horrible with names, mostly because I doubted myself with them, so I begged my guides to be precise. "Bill. His name is Bill," I heard.

As nonchalantly as I could I walked past Bill, stopped, and looked at him. "Bill?" I asked, pretending to recognize him. I was an awful liar, so I was hoping that I wasn't so translucent.

The man wiped his tears and looked up at me in question.

"Bill, I am so sorry. I heard about Peg. My mom had been friends with her," I lied, hoping I would be forgiven. "She fought such a tough battle."

"For years," he replied, taking out a handkerchief and blowing his nose. "Damn cancer."

I nodded back in understanding.

"You know I really believe that they hear us in Heaven. The more you talk to her, the easier it gets. And I know that it isn't the same as them being here with us, but it does help to get us through the bad days. It helps me with my mom at least."

Bill bent his head and began to cry again.

"Tell him I send him pennies," Peg told me.

"Have you ever heard of pennies from Heaven?"

Bill raised his head up, his green eyes still sparkling with tears, and looked at me oddly. He reached inside his pocket and brought out a penny. "When I sat down on this bench, I found it just lying there. I thought maybe it was a sign from her and then thought that was just silly."

"What year is the penny?" I inquired, hoping that my intuition was right.

"What?" he puzzled.

"Just curious as to what the date of the penny is. I heard that if you find a coin in a conspicuous place that sometimes the date is relevant. I just thought maybe…"

"What the he…?" Bill stammered as he looked at the dulled copper coin. "1955." He looked up at me. "Our wedding anniversary year." His tears began again.

"She hears you, Bill. I'm sure she hears you. Keep talking to her. Mourn, but celebrate with her that she no longer hurts. I do believe that pennies are your sign. And that they are from Heaven."

I looked over at Peg, who was crying but smiled a thank you at me through her tears.

Bill rose from the bench and I gave this complete stranger a hug. Not from me but from Peg; he just probably didn't know it.

As I walked away, I realized that it wasn't a coincidence that my headphones were missing. Or that I walked that way that day at that time and had to stop for a leg cramp. We are so often placed in situations, at certain times, with certain people, to complete certain quests, but we are so caught up in our world that we don't see it. Or hear it. And most of the time we don't do it.

Take some time in your busy schedule to look and listen around you—*really* look and listen around you. We receive messages from the Other Side all the time. Or those from this side offering us messages. Are you listening? Do you hear them? Are you paying attention to your pennies from Heaven?

Chapter Five
Guidance from the Other Side

I have had sessions with clients who have had horrific experiences, and I am always in awe at their strength. When I ask them how they got through the sadness and the chaos of the situation, the answer is typically the same: You do what you have to do to find peace within, to just get through it.

Not All Who Wander Are Lost

"This is Kristy," I answered my phone.

"Kristy Robinett?" the lady on the other end questioned.

"Yes," I responded, thinking that it was more than likely a salesperson. And since I rarely to never answered my phone I was wondering if I was going to regret answering it then.

"Kristy, this is going to sound crazy." I heard the lady take a deep breath. "I think my house is haunted and wondered if you could help me."

"Wait...let's start with what your name is." I smiled into the receiver.

I sensed her smile back. "I'm sorry," she giggled nervously. "My name is Kim and I live in the Novi, Michigan, area."

I receive calls from all over the United States and Canada from those claiming to be a victim of a haunting. Obviously I can't travel everywhere, but seeing as Kim was local and I had a couple of hours to spare the following day, I grabbed her address and promised to visit her.

"I am so relieved," she sighed. "I feel like I'm going crazy!"

The next day, I pulled up to the colonial home that sat in the middle of a nice suburb, put the car in park, turned off the ignition, closed my eyes, and grounded myself. Grounding, or securing and tethering your energy, is important so that the information received is coming from the proper place. Have you ever just sat in a room where many people were talking and you felt yourself wander and couldn't figure out what anyone said? That is being ungrounded.

I opened the car door, grabbed my purse, and made my way to the large red front door that was decorated with a beautiful grapevine wreath. I didn't even have to ring the doorbell when a pretty lady opened the door and introduced herself as Kim and invited me in.

I immediately saw the spirit of a lady who was the spitting image of Kim, only older, standing behind her. I smiled; it was a much simpler case than I could have hoped.

I sat across from Kim on her couch in her family room that overlooked a small creek. It was quite peaceful and not at all the way some houses I have investigated felt.

"My alarm clock continues to go off at 4:30 a.m. every single morning, Kristy. No matter what I do. I even bought a new one, and sure enough, it went off too. And my coffeemaker has been randomly making coffee. I set it for the morning, but every so often I will be sitting here and I will smell coffee, only to find that the coffee has been brewed."

I nodded as I looked over at the older lady in spirit who was sitting next to Kim, smiling mischievously.

"I even called an electrician out who said that there was absolutely nothing wrong. But before he left, he said he heard a whisper and maybe I had a ghost! I laughed because I thought he was joking, but he was dead serious. He gave me your business card."

I raised my eyebrow and laughed. I always found it interesting as to how people come upon my information.

"Kim, has your mom recently passed away—been gone less than a year?"

Kim looked at me with her large green eyes and nodded.

"She had a stroke, right, and you had to take her off of life support?"

"How did you … ?"

"You aren't being haunted, Kim, you are just getting your hello from Heaven. Your mom is actually sitting next to you, by the way..."

Kim looked at me and then next to her in hopes she would see her.

"She says that you keep wondering if you did the right thing."

Kim began to cry and nodded her head. "Oh, yes, I wonder that every night when I go to bed."

"You did the right thing," I quietly replied. "So your mom is just trying to reassure you of that. As for the coffee, she's just trying to be helpful. The alarm time has something to do with a birthdate."

Kim wiped her tears. "My birthdate is April 30th!!"

"So that would just be her saying she's happy you are her daughter."

I immediately heard her mom say, "*Not all who wander are lost.*" I repeated it to Kim and she laughed.

"Mom would say that all of the time. Maybe it needs to be changed to 'Not all who haunt are ghosts.'" Kim thought for a moment. "So it isn't a ghost?"

"Nope it's just your mom and she isn't a ghost. Recognize her, talk to her, but most of all forgive yourself for what needs no forgiveness—her journey was her journey and you should take no responsibility for it."

Ninety-five percent of so-called paranormal cases that I am called on to help with tend not to be a ghost at all, but a spirit. Ghosts are those that haven't crossed over, while a spirit is someone who has crossed, but comes to visit. And most of those visiting are family members, friends, and sometimes nosy neighbors who may have lived in the house, on that land, or near the house and land.

Kim called me several months later to tell me that the coffeepot still brews by itself every so often, and the alarm goes off, but not as much as before. But most of all she called to tell me that she had forgiven herself and felt comforted in knowing that her mom is still around her. "I think I was just so ungrounded with everything going on that I didn't take into consideration that it was Mom!"

The Wedding Dress

"Patty, you have to seriously consider this. You are far too exhausted to do this alone," the man with the silver hair and gentle brown eyes said to her as he lovingly touched her right shoulder and walked out of the hospital room.

Patty looked over at the frail woman lying in the bed. It was hard to see the mom in her any longer. And even harder to believe that the woman, who looked like she was an ailing eighty-plus-year-old, was only sixty years old and dying. Patty glanced at the pamphlet Dr. Tuttle had given her and shuddered—"End Your Life Graciously and with Dignity with Hospice."

Gloria had complained of headaches for years, but neither Patty nor her mom had suspected anything like this. The cancer was diagnosed only three weeks prior. Stage 3 brain cancer. The doctors were trying treatment, but Patty wasn't sure if the treatment would kill her mom first, or the cancer. But she knew that no matter what, her mom would not survive long.

Patty's workplace was sympathetic, but she had used all of her sick and vacation days and was left with zero paid time off and bills to pay. And then there were her two sons who needed her too. Patty's ex-husband had begrudgingly taken on a full-time role, but his patience was also wearing thin. She was stuck between a rock and a hard place.

"Are you still here, Pat?" her mom's weary voice called.

"Of course I am, Mom. What can I get you? You want me to call for a tray?" Patty asked while wetting a white washcloth and gently laying it on her mom's sweaty forehead. The medication they were giving Gloria was like hell water. She shivered, but was feverish at the same time. Patty only wished that she could shiver the cancer away, but she knew that was just silly.

"No, I'm not hungry. You need to go get the boys. Go spend time with them. I promise that I won't die on you yet." Gloria slyly grinned, but the lighthearted, albeit a bit macabre moment only lasted a second before she started dry heaving into the small bedpan the nurse had left on the end table. "Go. I mean it, Pat. At least go home, shower, and sleep. How are we supposed to find you a cute doctor with you looking that way?"

Patty rolled her eyes and smiled. She always loved her mom's wicked sense of humor. And there was rarely a time when Gloria didn't try to match Patty up with someone. The day after Gloria's diagnosis, she looked straight in her daughter's eyes and told her that either in life or death, she would find that special someone for her, because she felt that Patty deserved that.

Patty's father was her mom's soul mate. Gloria and Bill were married at the tender age of nineteen and just a year later welcomed their only child, Patricia Jean Schultz. They spent almost every single moment with one another until Bill died unexpectedly just five years previously. Bill loved giving back and helping out as a volunteer firefighter. It was a cold winter night when he got a call that a local restaurant had caught fire. A few hours later Gloria received the grim news that the roof of the burning building had collapsed on Bill, killing him instantly. Gloria was a survivor, though, and she believed in life after death. "Faith will get us through this, Patty," she would say.

Patty wasn't so sure. The loss of her father came the same year as the loss of her marriage. She was so devastated that she changed her name back to her maiden name despite friends and family telling her she was being ridiculous, but to her it was the only way to keep her dad close to her. The only way.

Patty had lost faith and became bitter, despite having great children. Her life became like the movie *Groundhog Day*: wake up, get the kids ready for school, drop the kids off at school, go to work, come home from work, get the kids ready for bed, go to bed, and repeat the next day. She was living to die, not living to live. And her mom knew it, often pestering her to move on.

"Why don't you go out on a date, Patty. You are so pretty. And so smart. Just because you married and divorced a dud doesn't mean that better ones aren't out there."

Patty would scowl at her mom and ignore the comment. But she was afraid of failing again. It was easier her way.

"Well, one day I am going to fix you up with someone and force you to go out on that date," Gloria would warn. "I know Dad wants that too."

"Wants? Dad is dead, Mom. He can't do anything for you, for me, for his grandkids. He's gone."

Patty's cynicism never got to Gloria. It was her time to ignore the skepticism. "You'll see one day, Patty. You'll see."

Patty shook her head, realizing that she was more tired than she thought. "A shower and some sleep sounds good, Mom. But if you need anything, call me, or have the nurse call me as soon as possible, okay?"

Patty reached down and kissed her mom's forehead. She smelled of baby powder. Gloria always smelled of baby powder.

On Patty's way to the car the guilt took over. Even though she so badly wanted a hot shower and some sleep, her mom was fighting for her life and that trumped everything. Including Patty's job that had left four voice messages, all inquiring when her return date would be.

Patty's home phone was ringing as soon as she walked in the door. She tossed her keys on the dining room table that had three weeks of unopened mail on it, and she picked up the phone.

"Hello?"

"Ms. Schultz?"

Patty held her breath, praying it wasn't that call. "Yes, this is Ms. Schultz, what can I help you with?"

"This is Maria from I Do Again. Oh, we are so glad to finally get a hold of you. We've been trying all week. Your wedding gown is in and ready to be picked up anytime," the female voice said in an upbeat and positive tone.

"I'm sorry, there must be a mistake," Patty exclaimed.

"This is Patricia Schultz?"

"Umm, yes, but I can assure you that I have no wedding dress to pick up. Not even a man to marry in a wedding dress," Patty laughed.

"That is incredibly odd. I have your name as Patricia Schultz and this phone number. They show the wedding date is ... let me check for sure. Yes, here it is—April tenth, six months from today."

Patty sucked her breath in. April tenth was her mom and dad's wedding anniversary date. How very strange and coincidental, she thought, baffled at it all.

"I am so sorry, but you must have me mixed up with someone else. It isn't my dress."

Her cell phone chimed just then and she saw it was the hospital calling.

"I have to go. I hope you find the rightful owner." Patty hung up the landline and answered the singing cell.

"Patty, this is Dr. Tuttle. Your mom passed away about fifteen minutes ago. We tried everything, but she was already gone. I'm so sorry."

Patty wasn't even sure what made her laugh and think that her work would be happy to know she would probably be back to work the next week, but that was her first thought before she collapsed on the floor and sobbed. "Mom, you promised you wouldn't die. I knew I shouldn't have left. You promised!"

The wedding dress call was all but forgotten.

Gloria was a planner and after Bill died, she had planned and paid for everything for when it was her time. She was always very organized and tidy, making it very easy on Patty. And although through the years they would bicker that Gloria bordered on obsessive compulsive behavior with her ultra-tidiness, Patty was more than grateful for it in this predicament. And just four days later she returned to her workplace, as if the last month hadn't even happened.

Patty worked as an IT manager at a large public company, where she was more of a number than a name. She took calls throughout the corporation, from problems with printers to death-blue screens on computers. She set up presentations for the executives and dispatched her team accordingly. There weren't many women in her field and she was good at it and knew it. Just a couple of days after her mom's funeral, her assistant Janet handed her a pile of resumes.

"We have been authorized to hire two more team members," Janet said. "Your first applicant will be here in about a half hour and then there are four more every half hour after. I already called lunch in for you. You look like hell and need to eat." Janet breezed out of the office as quickly as she breezed in.

Patty laughed. She was grateful for Janet and her bluntness. They made a great team. Most people would be offended, but not Patty. The person who sat just a few feet from her for more than eight hours a day, five days a week, for more than ten years, had never asked once how she was— not even after her dad's or her mom's passing. Instead Janet knew that Patty was a grown woman and that she wasn't her confidante; she was her assistant. They got one another.

After the third candidate's interview, Patty threw the portfolios on the desk. Any of them would do just fine. She knew that she was numb, but it did feel good to get back into the office and into a routine, even if it was a bit like *Groundhog Day*.

"Ms. Schultz, your final candidate is here," Janet said as she led a tall and thin-built man into her office. *He must be 6'4",* Patty thought, trying not to stare as she stood to greet him.

Patty shook the stranger's hand. "Call me Patty. Please have a seat."

"I'm Bill," the man introduced himself as he sat in the gray tweed office chair across from her.

Patty tried not to act distracted as she conducted the interview, but she couldn't get over the odd connection she felt to Bill. Despite sharing the name with her father, there were lots of Williams and Bills, she discounted, but there was something so comfortable about him.

Before the interview was done, Janet walked in with two sandwiches and a bag of chips and put them on the desk. Patty was shocked. "Janet, I am not done yet. This can wait."

Janet smiled at Bill. "I am sure you are already hired. You see she just lost her mom and she needs to eat. If you eat with her, she will eat, I'm sure of it."

Before walking out of the room, Janet winked at Patty, making her blush.

"I am so sorry for the unprofessional behavior. That is not like my assistant at all," Patty apologized.

"No apologies needed. I just lost my dad last year," Bill said. "I get it. Why don't we eat and just talk about non-business things? Or we can eat and talk about hard drives if that makes you more comfortable," Bill joked mischievously.

Patty stared at him for a split second, trying to conjure an excuse about her being the boss when she caught a strong scent of baby powder. She glanced around to see where it came from, but nobody had walked by. The smell made her think of her mom and for a moment she thought perhaps Bill was Heaven-sent and she laughed. Just a silly coincidence, she reasoned.

But it was odd because Patty felt something. After so many years, Bill made her feel something and the oddest thing was it didn't frighten her. They spent over two hours talking about their families, their divorces, and their favorite vacation spot—which ironically was at the exact same place: Charleston, South Carolina.

Patty hired Bill on the spot, along with another candidate she had interviewed, but couldn't quite put a finger on what she was going to do. She couldn't possibly have feelings for a stranger who was now her employee, after just a couple of hours. Could she?

Bill felt it too, and refused to accept her excuses for not going out with him. There was nothing in the employee handbook that made it illegal or unethical for them to date, and after a lot of pestering and begging, Patty agreed to a Friday night date. And every Friday and Saturday night for the next two months, until on New Year's Eve, right at midnight, Bill got on bended knee and proposed to Patty with her sons by her side. And she said yes, without any doubt in her head.

"I don't want anything big in the way of a wedding," Patty would say. "Just something simple."

But her girls pestered her to get a wedding dress, even just a simple one. Her mom, their grandma, would've wanted it that way. So when she stopped into the bridal shop close to her office, she laughed at the name—I Do Again, and then thought of the call she received right before her mom passed away.

"Can I help you?" the middle-aged lady with short blond hair asked.

Patty started babbling about a small wedding and a simple dress when the saleswoman laughed, "First, let's start with your name. I'm Sophie."

Patty laughed and apologized, "My name is Patty Schultz and I am looking for a simple gown. Second time's the charm, right?"

Sophie looked at Patty as if she had seen a ghost before asking her to repeat her name.

"Patty Schultz." Patty repeated. "Do we know one another?" she asked, confused.

"That's what I thought you said. I think I called you several months back about a dress that you never picked up."

"You never found the owner?" Patty exclaimed.

"Give me a moment, please," Sophie said and briskly walked into the backroom. A couple of minutes later she came out carrying a white bag over her arm. "Let's try this on for giggles."

Patty was confused, but followed Sophie into the large fitting room. Sophie motioned for Patty to step up on a stage-like pedestal surrounded by a three-way mirror. As Patty undressed, she caught a glimpse of the gown in the mirror as Sophie unzipped the bag. It was beautiful. Simple. Elegant. And exactly what she was looking for.

Sophie slipped it over Patty's head and they both gasped. The fit was perfect and Patty began to cry as she looked at herself in the mirror. It wasn't just the dress, it was that she never thought she would ever again believe in love. In marriage. In this. And she wished her mom could see her now.

"But I don't understand," Patty said to the saleswoman. "How? I just recently met my fiancé." Before she could finish her sentence she caught sight of the signature on the receipt that was stapled to the gown's bag. It was obvious to her that it was her mom's writing. She always knew that her mom was organized, but this was a bit excessive, yet much appreciated.

"Unbelievable," Sophie responded after Patty finished explaining everything to her. "Well, it is paid for and all yours. A gift from Heaven, you might even say."

And just like that Patty smelled the scent of baby powder and she knew that nothing was truer.

Making Peace

"I just want peace." Delores folded her hands in her lap and looked up at me with her honey brown eyes.

It had been a rough few years for the sixty-something southern belle. Originally from Georgia, she had lived for several decades in Michigan, but kept her accent. Both of her parents passed in a car accident, together. Although that gave Delores some peace—knowing that they were together—even before their bodies were in the ground, a huge fight with her three siblings ensued regarding her parent's estate. A family that through thick and thin, until then, had stuck together, was now torn apart and words were spoken that could never be forgotten and probably not forgiven.

"And what is it that brings you peace, Delores?" I asked her.

She wrinkled her nose at me, as if I had asked her to eat food she disliked.

"All I know is that my life is filled with chaos and I am losing myself, my marriage, my children...my sanity. I just want peace," she repeated firmly. "And I miss my parents," she said solemnly.

"If you don't know what brings you peace, how will you ever find it?" Now, I am not Confucius, but I do believe that it is the times when we are the most lost, the times when we are going through the most chaos—when we discover the secrets within our souls. Sure, we may cuss those times, wonder and moan why we were ever thrown into the horrible situation, but once the dust has cleared, more times than not we come out with life lessons that help us. Or help others.

"Delores, close your eyes and see yourself happy—describe it."

"I see my family gathered around a dining room table."

"Do you smell anything?"

"Yes, I can smell popcorn."

"What are you doing?"

"We are laughing about a silly joke one of the kids told."

Delores opened her tear-filled eyes. "So my peace is the very thing that is making me nuts?"

"Not exactly, but you now know that you feel peaceful when the family is together, getting along…and there is popcorn involved."

We both started to laugh.

"But really, do you know why you smell popcorn? What does that have to do with your mom and dad?"

Delores wrinkled her nose at me again, but contemplated for a couple of minutes. "I didn't realize that the thoughts of my mom and dad give me peace. My mom would make us popcorn every Friday night. It was always a fun occasion. And then I was a teenager and it wasn't important to me. I guess it is more important than I thought."

"When you find peace within yourself, you become the kind of person who can live at peace with others. And again, popcorn might make it better too."

Delores checked in with me a few months after her appointment and said that she started the Friday night popcorn and movie night with her family and felt close to both her parents and her family again.

I suggested that Delores start a daily journal to note the positive things, the things that made her feel satisfied, and to start her day with thoughts of peace and end her day with the same. Peace is rarely about material things, but finding peace in simple moments.

Common signs the Other Side sends from the animal kingdom include butterflies, dragonflies, birds, ladybugs, squirrels, and chipmunks, but really the list is endless and sometimes very imaginative. You'll soon read about the young man who sent his mom spiders after he passed. It isn't that your loved one is reincarnated as that insect or animal, but just that they send their energy to that insect or animal. You will know it is a sign if that animal or insect acts unusual, such as landing on you, continuously pecking at your window, staring and not moving, "talking" by screaming or making an incessant noise. They try to make it obvious so that you don't doubt; take that minute to stop and pay attention so they can let you know they are still there and they are with you.

Pay attention to an animal that acts unusual, like a butterfly that just won't leave you alone, or your pet that keeps staring into the corner of the room, or maybe you are constantly finding ladybugs in unusual places. Animals are very in touch with the spirit world and are good indicators that spirit is around, or are helping to offer a Heaven hello.

Duck Duck

Many times there is a reason behind the animal our loved ones show us, as it might have been a favorite of the person who has crossed over, but sometimes it doesn't make complete sense as to why it was *that* specific animal or insect—at least until later.

I had a client in my office who was very adamant about speaking to her mom who had passed over ten years before. Dottie's mom came through with very motherly advice. She was concerned her daughter was always in a constant hurry, stressed, and she actually called Dottie sassy. "Stop and smell the roses," her mom emphasized, which was met with Dottie giving me an attitude.

"She says that the ducks are important. The six ducks, to be exact."

"I don't have a clue what that means, Kristy," Dottie said, irritated.

"Are there six of you? Did your mom have six children?"

"Well, yes, but what do the ducks mean?"

I shrugged my shoulders after her mom didn't offer me any more clarity. I pulled out a favorite book of mine by author Steven Farmer, *Animal Spirit Guides.* "Steven often speaks of ducks as a reminder to reconnect with family. Ducks also help with uneven emotions and feeling overwhelmed. So I suppose that is a complimentary message, right?"

Dottie didn't think so. In fact, I think she thought I made it all up, and while she left my office gracious, I could tell she was peeved. I was used to being the scapegoat—after all, the messenger typically is, even the messenger to the Other Side—but I strive for my clients to leave with messages and with answers—not more questions.

The feeling of letting her down in some way stayed with me through the remainder of the day. On my way out the door, I threw my light jacket on, grabbed my purse, and as I was going to throw my cell phone into the pocket of my purse I noticed that I had a voice mail. I hit play.

"Umm, Kristy, this is Dottie. I just wanted to let you know that the ducks make sense."

I heard her take a deep breath before she began again. Her voice was shaky and it sounded like she might have been crying.

"When I left your office, I was upset. Mom was never a good communicator, and I don't know why I thought that would be any different. I was running late for work and got stuck in traffic, but I didn't know why—there were two cars in front of me just stopped and I couldn't figure it out, so I started honking my horn when I noticed what the holdup was. There was a momma duck and her six ducklings crossing the road. Six ducks," she repeated. "Thanks, Kristy, and I'm sorry I was a sourpuss and probably rude. Apparently, Mom really wanted me to know that she really is around me. So I will reassess my patience… and call my siblings. Thanks again."

I smiled into the phone. Our loved ones don't have vocal cords like we do and I often describe my interactions with them like playing charades. I am human and sometimes I don't completely understand what they are showing or telling me; it can be lost in translation. But Dottie's mom was adamant about ducks and it was a message for the future, not one about the past. Just like the dreams that we have, their maeesages have symbolic meanings entangled and sense has to be made out of nonsense. Sometimes it happens quickly, sometimes it doesn't.

Insects

I was doing a séance at a Halloween event when a young male came through in spirit and told me to tell his mom that he sent her spiders. I could feel spider webs tickling my face and what felt like spiders crawling up my arm. I wanted to shriek, but I had previously instructed everyone to keep their fingertips on the table and to not break the circle. I didn't want to be the defiant one, so I squinted and winced, hoping that nobody was watching me in the dimly lit room.

A woman started to cry but laugh at the same time. "That would be my son. He said that if he ever died, he would send me spiders to scare me. And he does!" she exclaimed. "I am constantly finding small spiders in the house and we never had them before Joshua died. I know that it is him letting me know that he is there and teasing me at the same time."

After my husband lost his father, he started to notice dragonflies. They wouldn't just fly around him, but actually land on him and stay until he moved them away. One afternoon when the family ventured out to a local Renaissance festival, we were walking down the uneven dirt path when we all stopped and stared at Chuck. He had five dragonflies land on him simultaneously, and they comfortably sat on his arms and shoulders. And the reason? Just a friendly Heaven hello.

I often get inquiries as to the why. Most people think it must be a message that denotes a warning or impending doom. But most times it is merely just a hello and nothing more than that.

Dragonfly Memories

Jodi came to me just a week after her daughter Abby made her transition to the Other Side. Although I typically tell my clients to wait a year before they visit me after a loved one has passed, Jodi had scheduled the appointment a year before to talk to her dad, whom she lost when she was young. At the time the appointment was booked, never in a million years had Jodi thought she would be sitting in my office with the hopes of talking to her baby girl.

"Life goes on, that is what they keep telling me," she cried. "But how could it? I still miss my dad after all of these years, and how can the wounds of losing a child ever heal?"

I didn't know how to answer her. I knew from past client experiences that she was right. A new life was built without the child, but the wounds never really healed.

I was surprised when a pretty little girl with long brown hair and wearing a frilly pink party dress bounced into the office, hand in hand with her "Pa" and with a stuffed animal under her arm.

"Abby is right here, Jodi." I pointed. "And with her grandpa, your dad."

"But they never knew one another. How can that be?"

"On the Other Side, we know our family, our people. He says that he helped her cross over after the car accident. She has a stuffed animal, too, but I can't figure out what it is."

Jodi laughed, with tears running down her eyes. "That would be Hickory the Hippo. She never went anywhere without it. Once we lost it at the movie theater…" Jodi couldn't finish. "I don't think I can go on, Kristy. I only have pictures and memories, and what if they fade? They haunt my days and most of all my nights. I just want to be with her. With her and my dad."

"Life doesn't have to go on; it is a choice. A choice you will probably always contemplate, but you weren't taken, Jodi. It isn't yet your time. I don't know why you weren't taken and Abby was. I wish I had those answers."

"Why is my mommy crying?" Abby asked me. "I'm still here, it is just different."

I nodded at Abby, understanding that although she had only five earthly years, her Heaven years were much longer.

"I know that this is a lot to ask"—Jodi hesitated for a moment—"but would you go to the cemetery with me? It's just around the corner."

I was confused at the inquiry. I could see Abby standing right next to me and I wasn't sure what a cemetery field trip would accomplish, but Jodi's energy was insistent and I was really concerned with her mental state. Seeing that she was my only client of the day, I agreed. I sent a text message to my husband to let him know that I would be home a bit later than expected, along with a brief synapsis as to where I was going.

I followed Jodi's silver minivan, still with a booster seat inside, for about a mile, inside the gates to the cemetery and over to an area called the Lamb Garden, with rows and rows of burial sites for children. Before getting out of my vehicle, I closed my eyes and asked my guides to be with me, praying that the decision to come to the cemetery was the best thing to do and that my gift would be as clear as it was in the office. I wasn't sure, seeing that I was in a large cemetery.

The grass was still damp from the morning dew even though the sun had been shining for several hours. Jodi sat on the grass next to Abby's grave. I took my jacket, laid it down, and sat on top of it next to her.

"I should've taken that car," Jodi mumbled, pointing to the van. "The other car didn't have the booster seat in it and maybe that would've saved her." Jodi lay atop the plot. Freshly turned dirt was plastered to her right cheek as the tears moistened the soil into mud. Her cotton paisley-printed dress didn't do much to keep out the wind that was softly blowing around us, and she shivered a bit as she grabbed the bottle that was buried deep within her pockets. Without sitting up, Jodi counted out the small pieces. Fourteen in all, she confirmed. She put back the contents and with her hands shaking, she closed the lid.

"Abby, if you can help me and your mom right now, I would really appreciate it," I prayed, unsure what to do, what to say. Would holding Jodi help? Would calling my friend who is a therapist help? I just didn't know what to do except to ask Abby for a sign.

Movement startled us and just as the winged creature landed on Jodi's water-stained cheek, near her nose, I saw Abby come forward in spirit. The dragonfly contemplated both of us for a second, as if to say that we didn't belong here, before gently flying away. Its royal blue color matched Abby's eyes. Instead of feeling comforted by the divine creature, Jodi again broke into sobs, hugging the gray marble stone that portrayed her daughter's name: Abby Grace, age five.

As swiftly as the dragonfly had departed, it landed once again, and perched in front of Jodi. The moment rang serene as she looked up at the sunlight shimmering through its transparent wings and the coloring of its body, even more brilliant than seconds before.

"I've been asking for a sign, Kristy, some sort of sign, and have received nothing. Is this a sign or just a crazy coincidence?"

I often found it frustrating when signs so loud and so clear like this happened and yet were pushed away and discarded. "There's no such thing as coincidences, Jodi. Of course this is a sign!" Before I could finish my sentence, the dragonfly climbed on to Jodi's hand and without hesitation crawled upon her index finger and softly fluttered its wings before flying into the tree that hovered over the burial ground.

"Abby says that you have her candy with you," I whispered.

Jodi nodded and slowly rose to a sitting position. She took the bottle out of her pocket again and opened it. Emptying the contents into her hand, one by one she laid the colored M&Ms upon the tombstone; Abby's favorite candy.

"We were just going to run out real quick to get these. She had been good at school and I promised. I just wanted to keep my promise." Jodi fell into my arms.

"You did." I held the young mom, stroking her hair. "You did," I repeated.

Abby stood in front of us, just as she did in my office. "Tell her that I am sending her my baby sister. She's going to have blue eyes like mine and I hope she names her M&M!" Abby giggled and stroked her mom's hair with me as I delicately shared the message.

Jodi looked up and wiped her tears. "Nobody knows, Kristy, but I am pregnant. I haven't even told John yet!"

Eight months later I received a baby announcement, adorned with dragonflies.

Jodi and John are proud to announce their baby girl Emelia Madison. Inside a personal note read that she still sees dragonflies. She added that although she knew that Emilia wasn't Abby, she felt as if Em was touched by Heaven and that she would know that Abby was her big sister, forever.

Mourning Doves

Debi grew up with an incredible closeness to her maternal grandparents, Eileen and Bob. She was always with them. They lived in the same city, had a cottage where she spent every weekend, and on a couple of short occasions they lived with her family. They never missed an event, from First Communions and band concerts to birthday dinners and wedding showers, and they never missed being the first visitor after the birth of a baby—they were always there. They epitomized the word "grandparents."

As they grew older, they lived close to Debi's parents, who helped them with their everyday needs. Debi's grandpa passed away in 1998 and her grandma, Eileen, tried to live alone and did so for a short time until she had to have back surgery. Since the recovery would be lengthy, she and Debi's parents decided it would be best if she sold her condominium and moved in with them.

Debi's parents had a big kitchen in their house, which is on the outskirts of downtown Romeo, Michigan. An extra-large window offered a great view out the east side of the kitchen from the table, where her parents and grandma spent a lot of time because it was so open and airy. Shortly after her grandma moved in with her parents, a mourning dove appeared and spent each day sitting on the utility wire where he could see in that kitchen window. Her grandma named him Bob, after Debi's grandpa.

Bob sat on the wire every day, facing the house and looking into the window. In turn, her grandma looked back out at Bob and it was comforting for her to know he was close by.

Debi's grandma died on December 18, 2005. Heavy, wet snow was falling on the 21st, the day she was buried. The roads were slick and the funeral procession had to be rerouted (by Debi!) to avoid a slippery hill inside the cemetery. Since Debi was directing traffic at the front entrance of the cemetery, she had to literally run to the back of the cemetery when the last car passed so she wouldn't miss the graveside service. She ran frantically on the slippery cemetery road to get to the place where her grandma was being buried next to her grandpa.

Out of the blue, a car pulled up next to her. She never saw it coming, nor did she hear it coming. It just seemed to "magically" appear. The driver said he was from the funeral home, which was across the street from the cemetery and that he saw her directing traffic. The town was a small one and she didn't recognize him, but got in his car anyway. The man drove Debi to the back of the cemetery, without saying anything else, and dropped her off just as the service was starting. She quietly tucked herself under the large tent with the rest of her family.

Debi's good friend Kathy and her daughter Melissa were standing outside of the tent, braving the nasty weather to be at the service for Debi's grandma and, according to Kathy and Melissa, just as the priest finished his last blessing, a bird flew overhead, chirping loudly as if it was springtime. They said the bird flew so low they instinctively ducked and looked at each other in amazement that a mourning dove would be out in such horrible weather, let alone in wintertime in Michigan.

Shortly after her grandma's funeral, purple pansies began to grow next to the door of her parents' house. They popped through the snow and flourished as if the winter didn't exist. Pansies were Debi's grandma's favorite flowers.

Bob wasn't seen on the wire after Debi's grandma died. But from time to time every summer since then, a *pair* of mourning doves sit on the wire outside Debi's parents' kitchen window. And the pansies, sometimes purple and sometimes yellow, continue to fill the flower bed year after year where Bob and Eileen can sit and enjoy them while they are watched over by Debi's parents.

The Bluebird

"How do I know she hears me?"

"Oh, she hears you," I assured the young brunette who had her legs folded under her. Her mother in spirit walked over to the chair and sat down next to her, putting a reassuring hand on her daughter's shoulder.

The air, for a moment, turned crisp.

Brianna grabbed a tissue and hid her eyes from me as she broke down.

Her mom motioned for me to do something, so I sat down where her mom had been and held Brianna as she continued to cry.

"I didn't tell her that I loved her. I was an awful teenager. I didn't tell her that I loved her," she repeated.

Her mom informed me that it was true, Brianna had been an awful teenager, and then she laughed and said it was because Bri had a strong will and independence from the moment she gave birth to her. Her mom became melancholy and I could see the memories stirring between the two.

"Bri, your mom said she always knew that you loved her, during the good and the bad times. You should feel worse about stealing her car that one night just because a boy told you to."

Brianna erupted in laughter. "She told you that?"

I nodded.

"Does she know that I had a baby girl?" Brianna asked, clasping her tissue.

"And that she shares your mom's name? Yes, she knows." I smiled, reassuringly.

"Does she know that I can't seem to keep any relationships? I feel like such a failure."

"Nobody thinks you are a failure. You just involve yourself with the wrong types of men. And it started with the car fiasco," I repeated and grinned at her mom for trying to keep it lighthearted.

"Where is she?" Brianna looked around, as if trying to see what I could see.

"Right in back of you, Bri, but she's just a whisper away. She shows me a small bluebird."

Brianna looked at me curiously. "I don't know if I've ever seen one. Huh, I wonder what that means?"

I shrugged. "I'm not sure, but it is important. What are you doing in two weeks?"

"Going on a much-needed cruise." Brianna smiled.

"Good for you! I think it has something to do with that."

"Okay, not sure," Brianna skeptically answered. But three weeks later when I received an excited phone call from Brianna, it made sense.

"Kristy, you wouldn't believe it. Our ship was having problems and they had to give us another one. Its name? The Bluebird! And everything was themed around it, from the decorations to the nightly drinks. I felt mom with me the whole time. It was so special!"

So often we look for that physical thing to catch our eye loud and clear, but if your loved one says they bring you butterflies, it might not be a physical butterfly, but a note that has a butterfly on it, or a poem that someone shares with you that has a butterfly in it. Brianna got her bluebird loud and clear, but it doesn't always happen that way.

The Brown Horse

My husband, Chuck, was working in Michigan as a manager for a leading retail warehouse when he was asked to go to Kansas City to train for a new operating system. He was upset to be leaving his two small children behind, but his recent divorce had taken a toll on him and the change of environment would do him good. He called it a blessing. Even if it was just Kansas.

Chuck's Uncle Joe was his aunt's husband and not a blood relative, but that didn't matter because Uncle Joe was more like a father to Chuck than his own father. Joe was a man of large stature, with an honorable Irish heritage; he was a gentle giant unless he was crossed—and that was mostly only if he had been drinking gin. Joe McCusker was what many called an old soul; his wisdom and wide smile touched the lives of complete strangers. He was someone that legends were created about, and coworkers and family would often talk about how large his hands were and how it came in helpful at his job at Ford Motor Company, being that he could grasp more parts in his hand than a normal man. But this wasn't a legend, this was true. And Joe would have never even hurt a fly.

It was only two months after the cancer was discovered that Joe passed away, ironically on his favorite holiday, March 17, Saint Patrick's Day.

Uncle Joe was a father figure to Chuck in his most formative years and the grief from his uncle's passing stayed with him throughout his own adulthood. Chuck would often visit Joe's grave, take a swig of his favorite beer, and pour the rest on the gravestone, leaving that can as a means of love.

A few times a year, I hold séances. Although the term séance sounds ominous and spooky, there isn't much difference between my séances and a gallery reading, except I have three people come up to a small table and we do what is called table tipping.

Table tipping is a form of physical mediumship that dates back to the 1800s when the Fox sisters used it as a means of communicating with those on the Other Side. It allows participants the ability to see with their eyes or sense the communication as the table might tip, rotate, vibrate, and even sometimes levitate. Although I try to obtain messages for those at the small table, I also can receive messages from the loved ones of those in the audience.

In séances, a direct-voice medium, physical medium, or trance medium has the ability to allow those in the Afterlife to use their voice box in order to communicate, much like Whoopi Goldberg in the movie *Ghost*. Facial features may change and the medium's voice may change to that of the deceased. I have witnessed several of these types of séances and, to be honest, they are difficult to watch. The family members are often confused and thrilled at the same time, and the medium exhausted afterward. Needless to say, I am not a direct-voice or trance medium. Although it has happened to me before, I feel a loss of control over myself and I would much rather relay the information than become it.

Many times family members of mine and loved ones of Chuck's also come through, but I often push them aside so as to give the paying participants their messages. Spirit doesn't understand that. But it was at one of these séances when a man in spirit came through and said his name was Joe and showed his physical body on Earth with a towering height. I had a feeling from Chuck's stories that it was his uncle, but I had neither met him in life nor had a visit from him on the Other Side.

"Tell him I am showing you a four-leaf clover," Joe offered as validation.

"Yup." I could see Chuck nodding in the dim candlelit room.

"Tell him that I brought him the brown horse to show him that I am always with him."

"He mentions a horse, Chuck. And says that he brought you the brown horse to show you that he protects you," I repeated.

"The horse!" Chuck exclaimed. "Wow, I've often wondered who that was and what it meant!"

Chuck's grandparents on his father's side came from Bolckow, Missouri, a tiny town just an hour north of Kansas City, by the Nebraska border, population just a hundred-plus people. So while Chuck was working in Kansas City, he decided to explore his roots and look for the town cemetery to pay his respects to his ancestors.

The cemetery was down a State Road, on flat land. A tall wrought iron sign introduced the cemetery as *Bolckow Baptist Cemetery*. As he wandered the gravestones, he recognized many of the names from stories that his grandparents had told. Just as he started walking to his car, he heard a horse neigh. He looked up to see a house across the street with several horses grazing. But it was one brown horse that caught his eye, because the horse simply stood there staring at him, nodding, as if calling him over. So Chuck obliged and crossed the road, thinking at the same time that he must be nuts getting instructions from a horse, and hoping that their owner wouldn't come up with a shotgun thinking Chuck was going to steal one of the field horses. But he took the chance because he felt drawn in a way that could only be explained as divine.

Chuck asked the horse if he should know him, and the horse nodded and neighed to his questions, so that all Chuck could do was laugh in disbelief. He reached over and lovingly pet the large animal and asked if he could take a photo, of which the horse again nodded and seemed to pause in place as Chuck grabbed his camera from his coat pocket and snapped the shot. He didn't know why, but the horse moved him.

No other horse stepped close to the wooden fence except for this one and it felt like forever before he decided that his fear of being chased down a dirt road by the owner pointing a shotgun outweighed his amazement at the interaction. He said goodbye and went on his way, yet years later he thought of that large brown muscular horse and gazed at the photo that he took of it in Bolckow, Missouri. But the answer as to who it was and why didn't take place until over ten years later when his Uncle Joe came through in the séance.

"Tell him to always remember the horse," Joe reiterated.

You would've thought that the energy put into the horse would have come from one of his direct blood relatives, maybe someone who was laid to rest in the cemetery that he was visiting, but it didn't surprise Chuck or make him question. Instead, he felt that his Uncle Joe was like a relative, despite them not sharing blood and with Joe showing that he would forever protect and be with him, no matter the location and no matter the boundaries of life or death.

A Beloved Pet

Doug was so distraught at the loss of his father that the only thing he could do was keep himself busy and putter around his parents' yard.

Doug knew that at sixty-two years of age he was lucky to have his mother and his father; but his dad wasn't even ill and Doug didn't feel as if he was prepared. *Who is ever prepared for death?* he asked himself.

He looked around at his parents' retirement home. It was in Northern Michigan, in a town called Kalkaska, and although the touristy towns weren't far away, this was a slice of Heaven. No neighbors for several miles, and acre after acre of pine trees and lush hills; their land even had a small lake on it. The house wasn't anything special—just a modular home that his parents bought after his dad retired from Chrysler. It was simple, but perfect, and all the kids enjoyed traveling the three-plus hours each way once a month to visit. Not just for the serenity of the environment, but because Doug's parents were wonderful parents and grandparents.

Both of his parents emigrated from Russia. Anna and Niko treasured every penny they earned, and although they were generous with their children and grandchildren, they lived frugally, yet happily, without any regrets. The one thing they splurged on, other than their children, was their cherished dog, Sadie.

Sadie was Anna and Niko's prized beagle that their kids joked was treated better than they ever had been, and there was probably plenty of truth to that. A year previous Sadie had passed from stomach cancer and since that time, Doug noticed that his parents' typical laid-back personalities and smiles didn't go as deep. He was tempted to gift them a rescue puppy, but his parents kept saying that they were just too old to begin again with another dog. A year after Sadie passed, Doug's dad died. Doug was trying to comfort his mom on the death of her soul mate when he felt as if he himself might fall apart. All he could do to hold it together was putter on his father's tractor.

"Doug, why don't you come in for a sandwich," Doug's wife, Barb, called from the screen door.

Doug just shook his head and continued to work on the John Deere. Barb sighed and walked away from the doorway. She understood. She, too, had lost her own parents within the last few years.

Maybe a walk in the woods would help, Doug thought to himself. "I'm going to check out the deer stand," he shouted in the door to Barb, noticing that his mom was napping in his dad's favorite chair, a blanket wrapped around her. He shook his head and thought how life was unfair, and then beat himself up for the thought. He should be happy for the time he had. It was more time than many of his friends had with their parents.

Normally he would find comfort in walking the trails, but he was depressed and filled with grief. Everything reminded him of his dad. And then there were the questions on what to do with his mom. He couldn't leave her three-plus hours away from him, but he knew that it would be a fight to convince her to come back to city life. He just didn't know.

It was about a half mile to the tree stand where he and his dad had hunted for years. They never really caught much of anything. He always thought it was a way for his dad to get away from his mom, and maybe spend some quiet time. Thinking back at the conversation didn't bring comfort, but instead tears. Doug sat down on the ground in front of the tree stand and started uncontrollably sobbing. He didn't care that the ground was a bit muddy from the recent rain and that his pants were getting dirty. He didn't care about much of anything at that moment, but a rustling noise caught his attention.

Doug remained sitting, waiting to see if it was perhaps a deer coming to feed. Instead of deer, a squirrel, or chipmunk that was the typical wildlife, a small beagle puppy came out of the dense woods. Doug stared for a moment, and then gently called for the pup, who looked excited to see a human being. He came running and placed himself in Doug's lap. Doug laughed and looked around to see if the dog's owner was following, but after about fifteen minutes, Doug realized nobody was coming after him.

"You lost, puppy?" he asked, petting the small brown and white dog's head. He grabbed a piece of jerky he had in his pocket and fed it to the dog, who gulped it down as if he hadn't eaten for quite some time.

It didn't make sense, he thought. Neighbors were scarce and everybody knew everyone else's business and nobody had gotten a puppy. He couldn't just leave him in the woods, so he scooped the pup up and carried him back to his parents' house.

"Doug! What do you have there?" his wife exclaimed when he entered the door with the dog.

"I found him in the woods. He's probably lost. I'll drive into town to see if anyone's missing him."

"Doug?" His mom came into the front room, noticing the furry bundle he was holding. The puppy had fallen asleep in his arms, so he duly handed him to his mom. She sat down in his dad's chair and stroked the pup's head.

"I am going to take a shower and will run into town to see if he's missing," Doug repeated to his mom, but she wasn't paying any attention; she was smiling and crying while petting the dog.

"Mom?"

"Daddy sent him, Doug. Don't you see it?"

"Don't name him," Doug warned. "He has to belong to someone!"

After a hot shower, Doug ran to town and then to the local pet shelter, but nobody knew of a missing beagle puppy.

"Looks like he's all yours, Doug," Chip, the town bartender, said when Doug stopped in for a beer. "I bet you Niko sent him."

Doug smirked. "That's what mom said."

"And you don't believe that? After my mom passed away, we had a squirrel that kept trying to get into our house. It was the oddest thing. It wasn't until I acknowledged that mom sent the squirrel that the darned varmint stopped showing up."

On the ride home, Doug did something he had never done before. He turned down his radio and began to talk to his dad until he couldn't drive anymore. Tears blurred his vision, so he pulled over.

"Dad, I'm going to miss you. How am I supposed to go on without you? What am I supposed to do now?" Doug cried, knowing very well that he wouldn't get an answer, but the grief was pouring out of every bit of him. "And now this dog. Dad, I have to deal with Mom, and now a puppy? Did you really send him?"

Just as he asked his last question, his phone jingled. Looking at the number, he smiled and knew his answer. The screen said, "Dad calling."

"On my way home now, Mom," he said into the receiver.

Nobody ever called looking for the puppy. His mom named the dog Nicky after her husband, and they knew exactly why. He was Heaven sent.

Chapter Seven

Electronics and Phone Calls

It is common for electronic disturbances to occur when a loved one from the Other Side is near. Radios, televisions, cell phones, and just about anything electronic may turn on, turn off, or work incorrectly. Sometimes the Other Side is able to use these items as a means to communicate to their loved ones.

You More

Fifty years after graduating, high school sweethearts Carolyn and Andrew bumped into one another at a local restaurant. It was like love at first sight all over again. Both had been married and divorced once before, and although the relationship progressed into a serious one, it was decided that they would live independently and without participating in a traditional marriage. They both had older children and were retired from good jobs, but they missed the companionship. Everyone who saw them together commented how romantic it was, and Carolyn and Andrew agreed. They were madly in love.

Carolyn loved Andrew's outgoing personality. No matter where they went, it seemed someone knew Andrew and always had a kind word to say. They shared similar interests and became inseparable, meeting every morning for breakfast and most every evening for dinner. When Andrew didn't show up at the local diner for their arranged breakfast date, Carolyn became worried. It wasn't like Andrew to stand her up. He was as dependable as the sunrise and sunset and that was one of the traits that attracted her to him, because it wasn't a quality that she had in her previous marriage.

They had just gone out with friends the night before; he dropped her off and kissed her on the cheek. Normally they would talk for a few minutes before bed, but she was tired and told him to just let the phone ring twice so she knew that he got home safe. When she heard the phone ring, she settled in for the night and peacefully slept.

Carolyn never failed to get excited to see Andrew, and that day she put on her favorite blue blouse and white linen slacks and made her way to their favorite breakfast place at exactly seven o'clock in the morning. But now forty-five minutes after the hour, the petite lady asked the waitress if she might be able to use their phone.

After dialing Andrew's number and not getting an answer, she knew something wasn't right and she called Andrew's son. Paul only lived a couple of blocks from his dad and knew immediately from Carolyn's urgency that he needed to run over to check on his dad. Carolyn thanked the waitress, got into her car, and made her way over to Andrew's house. Maybe he had fallen down and couldn't get to the phone. *He probably tripped over the stacks of books he kept in his bedroom,* she thought. That had to be it. She kept telling him that he needed to let her unclutter his house.

By the time she got to the house, not only was Paul's car parked in back of Andrew's, but so was a police car and an ambulance—and she knew it was more serious than a trip and fall.

It was obvious that what made Carolyn fall in love with Andrew again impacted so many others. She had never seen so many people at a funeral before. His death was ruled a heart attack. His cell phone was lying on his stomach, but in the off position; Carolyn's number lit up when they flipped it open. They didn't believe he tried to call for help or anything with the way that his body was positioned. In the Medical Examiner's report it stated that Andrew more than likely just fell asleep and never woke up. It made Carolyn feel comforted to know that he didn't suffer, but she still wondered why his phone was with him. He typically left it on the charger through the night. It was a mystery that bewildered her. "Oh, he was probably just thinking of you," one friend suggested. "Maybe he forgot to tell you something and then just fell asleep," another offered. But she would never know for sure.

Carolyn didn't know how to grieve. She wasn't technically a widow without the marriage license or life insurance policy. Neither of which meant anything to her, but she was left without anything to attach herself to Andrew. No ashes, no last name, and not even an article of his clothing. His kids took everything and when she asked for a memento, they shrugged her off. Neither Carolyn nor Andrew were materialistic, and they never exchanged holiday gifts. It was the time they spent together that mattered, but the week following Andrew's funeral, Carolyn would have given anything to snuggle with a blanket, his shirt, anything of his. She was left with only pictures and memories.

Seven days after Andrew's funeral, Carolyn sat in her rocking chair staring out her patio window looking over her small vegetable garden. The June summer sun was teasing Carolyn's sun catchers and rays of rainbows shone on the carpet. She was lost in her thoughts when her phone rang. Glancing at the caller identification screen she noticed that the number was noted as restricted, but she answered anyway.

"Hello?" she said, her voice a bit weak from the past week of no sleep. At first nobody said anything and she thought maybe the line was bad, but just as soon as she went to hang up the phone she heard a crinkling at the other end and a voice came on.

"Carrie, its Andy."

A *cruel joke*, Carolyn, thought. How could someone be so cruel to pretend to be Andrew? "Who is this?" she demanded.

The male voice responded with just two words that made her believe she'd received a call from Heaven. "You more." And then the phone went dead.

She held the phone close to her ear hoping for another message, but nothing else came through. Then the recording came on reminding her that the phone was off the hook and needed to be hung up.

Carolyn and Andrew never said "I love you"; they both thought it was silly. Instead they would end their nightly phone conversations with "you more" and nobody ever knew it.

It was the most comforting sign and it was all hers. She was too afraid to tell anyone for fear they would judge her or think that dementia was setting in. That year after the call from Andrew, a few nights a week the phone would ring once or twice. Nobody would be on the other end and it was always from a restricted number. She called the phone company, hoping that there really wasn't an explanation other than something supernatural, and there wasn't. They didn't know where the phone calls were coming from. It gave her peace.

A year after Andrew's passing, she had to have a medical procedure that required her daughter Paula to spend a few nights with her. Paula settled on the couch the first evening. Sitting next to her mom they watched a reality singing show together when the phone rang.

"It's nine at night," Paula commented, reaching for the phone. Before Carolyn could tell her to just let it go, she had already answered. "Hello?"

Carolyn watched as Paula paled. "Who is this?" Paula demanded into the receiver.

Carolyn took the phone from her and set it down on the cradle without listening. "What did Andrew have to say tonight?"

Paula's eyes were wide as she shook her head in disbelief. "The man"—Paula choked—"Andrew, said 'watch Mom.' But how?"

Carolyn shrugged and continued to watch her program, ignoring Paula.

"Mom, how long has this person been calling you?"

Carolyn turned off the television. "*This person* is Andrew, and he has been calling since the week after his funeral. It isn't all the time; mostly at night he just lets the phone ring. Sometimes in the day I will answer and hear him breathe. I don't know how, but it is Andrew. Once I heard him laugh and it brought me comfort. End of story. I know you think I'm crazy…"

"I don't think you are crazy," Paula sighed. She didn't, but the message that she'd heard was foreboding.

"I'm really tired," Carolyn complained. "I think I'll go to bed."

Paula nodded and assisted her mom to her room. "Do you want me to sleep with you?"

"Don't be silly, I'm fine."

Carolyn was a stubborn gal, always was. Paula and her mom got along wonderfully when they weren't arguing, which was rare. As Paula got older she realized that they were just too much alike for their own good.

The next morning Paula got up and peeked in her mom's room to see her still in bed and panic took over. Carolyn would get up at five in the morning and it was almost eight. When Paula took a step into the bedroom, she realized Carolyn must have passed away during the night. The warning from the night before haunted Paula and she couldn't believe she didn't take it more seriously.

Carolyn's passing was ruled a blood clot caused from the recent surgery. It was only a couple days after her mom's funeral when the phone calls began at Paula's house. Just one ring and then nothing. As sad as she was, she knew her mom was now forever with her high school sweetheart and that they were probably so busy that the one ring was all Carolyn had time for, kicking it up in Heaven with her sweetheart.

Flashback

Thirteen-year-old Addison Logan from Wichita, Kansas, and his grandmother Lois spent a Thursday afternoon perusing several garage sales. Addison decided to purchase an old Polaroid camera marked for $1; it would end up being a supernatural shock when they got home. Inside the camera was a photo of Addison's uncle, Lois's son, Scott, who was killed in a car accident over twenty-three years before. Lois ventured back to the garage sale, but the man who held the sale couldn't remember where he had gotten the camera. After the surprise wore off, the family decided to take it as a sign from Heaven, from Scott himself, saying that he was doing okay.

In November of 2011, Tim Art received an e-mail from his childhood best friend, Jack Froese. Nothing surprising, as best friends often e-mail back and forth, except that Jack had passed away in June 2011 from a heart condition. The e-mail's subject said, "I'm Watching." The message read, "Did you hear me? I'm at your house. Clean your <bleeping> attic!!!" Froese used to continually tease Art about his messy attic. Not long after that, another e-mail from Froese came through to yet another friend, warning him of a pending ankle injury that actually happened days later. Instead of being spooked, Jack Froese's friends and family claimed that the e-mails were a gift from Heaven.

It was a balmy autumn day when Cindy stared out of her office window, wishing to be anywhere but where she was. It had been eight months since her husband had unexpectedly passed away after a minor procedure, and the grieving was still painful. Her work e-mail pinged, alerting her to new mail. When she glanced at her screen, her heart stopped. The e-mail was from her husband, with the e-mail subject, "Missing You." The content of the message simply read, "I really miss you today. Love you lots." Stunned but grateful for the message, she picked up their wedding photo, stained with tears, and kissed it, whispering, "I miss and love you too." When alive, her husband would send her a morning e-mail when he got to work.

Could the e-mails have simply been caught up in a server and just delivered late? Sure, but regardless, experiences such as these happen daily. Many chalk it up to coincidence, or are skeptical about the legitimacy of the stories, while others (including me) believe that it is pure synchronicity. They all happened at the right time.

Sparkle

Her name was Suzie, but everybody called her by her nickname, Sparkle. She was always extroverted, with a friendly and engaging smile and warmth that would've made anyone think she was a schoolteacher or nurse, and most definitely a mom, but she was none of those.

Her life started out shaky. Born to an unwed and very young mother, Sparkle was placed for adoption, in hopes of her having a better life. But Sparkle's adoptive family was far from what her biological mother could've ever wished for her. Her adoptive mother had a drinking problem, and her adoptive father was physically and emotionally abusive. He molested her from the age of five until she ran away from home at sixteen. She lived on the streets and became addicted to alcohol and drugs—anything to numb her emotional and physical pain. The abuse had been so terrible that she developed an infection that required an emergency hysterectomy at the age of twenty, so there would be no biological children for Sparkle.

It was in the hospital, after her surgical recovery, that a nurse took a fondness to the pretty blond-haired, blue-eyed girl's spirit and began inquiring about her life and her life expectations. When Suzie told her of her past, the nurse fumed and asked to get law enforcement involved, but Sparkle only shook her head and said that she would much rather find heal-ing—somehow, someway. This is how I got to know Sparkle.

Emily, the spunky nurse with short brown hair and gray eyes, had been a long-time client of mine, and after Spar-kle was released from the hospital, Emily took her into her own home, with several strict stipulations—no drinking, no drugs, no men, and she had to go to counseling and AA every single week. It was the first time that anyone had taken a chance on the young girl with a checkered past, and she grinned from ear to ear, promising to do everything Emily asked of her. Most young adults would be irate over rules, but Sparkle never had any, and to her it felt like someone actually cared. Emily had her reservations and even asked me during one of our sessions if I thought she was making a mistake. I didn't see a mistake, I saw a perfect fit.

For five-plus years, Emily helped Sparkle find self-love and healing, and Sparkle helped Emily just as much as Emily helped Sparkle. Emily had lost both her parents, her hus-band had left her after their kids went off to college, and she was sick.

Emily didn't want anybody to know how severe her ail-ments were, especially her employer. Anytime she came to my office and I mentioned her health issues, she would wave me off, saying that we were all going to die at one point, and in-stead wanted to hear about a potential love interest, or a win-ning scratch-off ticket. We would laugh and I would honor it. I loved giving her sessions, and sometimes she would bring Sparkle and I could see the love between them—the mother that Sparkle never had. So I was excited to see Emily's name on my schedule, and yet surprised when Sparkle instead walked into my office—tears streaming down her face.

"Kristy, she passed away a couple weeks ago."

I held Suzie and we both cried, and then laughed at the thought of Emily yelling at us for crying.

"I found out a couple months ago that I have cancer. I never told her, because she would've used all of her extra energy to fight for me."

And we cried again.

"Has Emily given you any signs?" I inquired.

"Actually, yes," Sparkle grinned. "It was an hour after she passed away when I received a phone call with a restricted number. I thought it was odd, but I answered it anyhow thinking maybe it was one of Emily's kids. But nobody was there. I could sense someone there, but nobody spoke. There was nothing," she repeated.

I raised my eyebrow and looked behind Sparkle, where I could see the spirit of Emily standing. Her expression radiated concern, but before I could get a feel for what it was, Sparkle continued.

"The restricted numbers have continued. I get them at different times during the day and night, but just recently they have come more frequently. I even went to the cell phone shop and they have no explanation. They say that it isn't showing up on their end. What do you think?" Sparkle asked.

I looked over at Emily, who nodded but also touched her chest, the same concerned look on her face.

"Absolutely, Sparkle, I would bet anything that it was Emily."

"That's what I thought. I heard that they could play with electronics, although I think it is odd."

As if on cue, Sparkle's cell phone that was sitting on the table lit up. No call or text showed up on the screen, it just glowed bright.

"You said you were sick? Is the cancer in the right breast?"

Sparkle nodded.

"And are you doing anything about it?" I asked, again looking at Emily who shook her head, as if answering for Sparkle.

"With everything going on, I just haven't had time. I have an appointment tomorrow, though."

Again the cell phone lit up, but no message of any kind showed.

"You promise to go, right? I know how much you dislike doctors and following instructions," I teased.

Sparkle laughed in response and promised that she would keep her appointment.

I asked Sparkle to keep in touch with me, and she promised she would, but just shy of a year after her appointment, I received a card in the mail from her husband with her funeral card in it.

And I cried.

Not because I was sad for her passing, but because I knew how much those two gals are kicking it on the Other Side and laughing!

Sparkle taught me so much, as did Emily. No matter what trials and tribulations there are, there is still a way to...well, SPARKLE.

It is easy for such sadness to make you negative, angry, sad, and even bitter, but I am reminded of a girl named Sparkle and the quote by noted psychiatrist and author Elisabeth Kübler-Ross: "People are like stained-glass windows. They sparkle and shine when the sun is out, but when the darkness sets in, their true beauty is revealed only if there is a light from within."

During your trials and your tribulations, and when you feel as if you are alone, know that there are sparkles within each one of us, even if you don't see them.

Chapter Eight

Spirit Encounters

A physical sighting is rare, but not uncommon. Most see their loved ones through shadows or sense them around, rather than seeing what paranormal enthusiasts call a full-blown apparition. Some will catch a glimpse of their loved one (or someone thought to look like their loved one) driving a car near them, or stopped at a red light. An easier way for our loved ones to come to us is through dream visitation.

A dream visitation is different than a typical dream as it very vivid, very peaceful, and very detailed. The visitation is remembered years later just as it is the morning after it happens. It typically occurs in color and you can make out every detail of your loved one, including their clothing and the environment that you are in. Sometimes they speak, sometimes they don't. Sometimes when they speak it comes in the form of telepathy, but not always. There is no hard and fast rule.

It has been estimated that the average person has 150,000 dreams by seventy years of age, but many of them are all but forgotten, which makes the waking dreams or visits the ones that are undeniably special.

I often receive inquiries from clients who've had so-called visitations with their loved ones, where they see their loved one in a casket, or their loved one is yelling at them. Rarely is a visitation hurtful. Many times these encounters are simply the regret that the person's subconscious mind is holding onto and not the real deal.

If you would like to have a visit with your loved one who's passed away, make sure to go to bed at a decent time and not exhausted, as it is imperative that you go through the proper sleep stages. Some believe that the Other Side can visit during the Alpha state, while others believe it is between the Delta and REM. Regardless of the science of it, transitioning properly through your sleep stages will help ensure a proper visit. There are many factors that can hinder a visit, and they include alcohol and several medications, including sleeping medications—but please don't stop taking prescription medicine without speaking to your physician.

Before you go to bed, make sure the temperature in the room is comfortable, and turn off the television or radio. Take some meditative deep breaths and think of the person you want to speak to, along with any questions you might want answered, and allow yourself to peacefully drift off to sleep. You'll find a "Visitation Meditation Before Bed" in the Appendix to help you further with this process.

As soon as you wake up, write down any and all images and messages that you may have received, even if they don't make any sense. You may have to do this for several nights, but the more that you dial the phone to your loved one, the more you are assured that during one of those calls, they will answer.

One of the easiest and most common ways that spirits communicate with us is through dreams and visits. Our conscious mind is turned down and our subconscious mind awakens, making it easier to visit with our loved ones. A true visit with your loved one in Heaven will be very specific and descript, and will give you peace and joy.

Chasing Mom

It was a dreary May morning when I woke up with my heart feeling sad, even though there wasn't any true and real reason to feel that way. I threw on my most comfortable t-shirt and black yoga pants, draped my favorite fuzzy red blanket over my lap, and sat staring out the window of my living room watching a comical show of a squirrel unsuccessfully trying to get into the bird feeder. I realized that my blue mood was because I was just missing my mom. There was no momentous day to make my heart ache for her. I could have blamed it on the gray sky or that Mother's Day was fast approaching, but it really had nothing to do with either of those things except that I just plain missed her.

"It must be nice to be a medium, you get to talk to your loved ones anytime you want." If only I had a dollar for every time I heard that. The reality is that every single person can talk to their loved ones. I had one person give me the *must be nice* line after a lecture I gave. I was signing my newest book for him when I looked up and asked him if he worked at a bank. He responded that he did, acting surprised that I knew that. "Must be nice to get as much money as you want, anytime you want," I said, smiling at him while I handed him the signed book. He got the point. Just because I can see, sense, hear, taste, and feel those on the Other Side doesn't make the missing go away, but it can ease it.

"Let's go shopping," my husband, Chuck, coaxed after noticing my case of the blahs.

"I don't really want to," I said, still staring out the window at the squirrel show.

"C'mon, it will make you feel better. I will even buy you something," he offered.

My mom loved shopping as much as my husband does, and with both of them born under the sign of Pisces, I felt that there was probably an astrological connection. *Well, Mom, I* thought teasingly, *I might as well go to the mall. You are probably there more than anywhere anyway.*

I've never been a shopper. Instead I am more of a "go and get what I want and get out of there" person. On the other hand, Chuck loves to look through racks of clothes and everything else. Most of the time it drives me crazy as it feels like wasted time. If you don't know what you need or want, how will you know by spending hours looking? My mom, though, was the same way as Chuck. At least until she lost her sight. She didn't grow up with much, and she made sure to take advantage of my dad's safe Ford Motor Company-with-overtime income. She shopped after she went blind, too, but it wasn't as much fun for her and she had to have an idea in her head as to what she wanted, because neither myself nor my dad were especially helpful in describing every piece of clothing to her as she decided whether she wanted it or not. So as much as shopping with Chuck was frustrating for me, it was also nostalgic of shopping with my mom.

The mall was not at all crowded while I followed Chuck to the second floor of a department store where he was looking for a new pillow and a Detroit Tiger t-shirt (at least this time he knew what he wanted!). After I looked around myself, and found nothing, I called out to Chuck that I would wait for him at the exit door. My bad mood was still clinging to me just as a lady cut in front of me to get on the escalator going down. I was looking at the moving stairs to make sure I didn't trip (I've always hated escalators), and it was a scent that caught my attention. The lady two steps down from me had on the same perfume that my mom used to wear. I looked up and was surprised to see that the lady in front of me was the spitting image of my mom; the clothes she was wearing, the coat she was wearing, her haircut ... everything was just like my own mom. I started to well up with tears when the lady turned to me and smiled and I about fell into her. It wasn't just someone that looked like her, it was her. She stepped off the escalator and hurriedly made her way through a jungle of clothes racks.

I didn't know what to do, or what to say, so I followed her at a close distance, all the while letting my tears fall. I wanted to go up to her and ask for a hug, but I was confused. My mom had been gone for several years, and although it would make sense that there was someone that looked like my mom, there was no mistaking that this was my mom. But how? I continued to follow her from a safe distance as she picked up clothes and looked at them, only to place them back down. Well, she wouldn't need clothes in Heaven, I kept thinking.

"Kristy?"

I turned around to see Chuck looking at me with a crooked look. I told him that I would be by the exit and instead I was hiding in the middle of Women's Wear.

"Look," I whispered to him and pointed to the lady. "She looks and smells like my mom! You do see her, right?"

Chuck nodded. "Yep, that's your mom alright. Sally!" Chuck yelled. "Sally Lou!" he yelled again, but the lady didn't react, she just continued to be entranced with all of the clothes.

"So I'm not crazy. She looks like my mom, right?" I asked, doubting myself.

Chuck nodded again in agreement. "So what now?" he asked.

I looked back at the lady, only to see that she was gone. "Where did she go?"

Chuck and I walked around the area, but nobody was there, only the faint scent of the perfume that I had smelled on the escalator. After two trips around the store, we realized that she was gone, and I reluctantly walked to the car, not sure how to feel. I just got the chance to see my mom. Not in spirit form, but to physically see her, and Chuck saw her too. I was excited, but still sad.

When I got home, I decided to share the story with my dad, a huge skeptic.

"And she was wearing that light brown leather coat that you bought," I chattered.

"Oh, so she was skinny Mom?" he sassed.

"Dad!" My mom's weight yo-yo'd a great deal and I was the most understanding of the annoyance as I seem to have inherited the same issue. She was, however, thin when I saw her in the department store. "Yes, she was thin Mom," I growled. "She had on blue jeans and a pretty pink sweater and just a bit of makeup. It was Mom," I reaffirmed.

"Then she just disappeared," Chuck added, shrugging his shoulders as if he didn't have any other explanation.

My dad didn't question me, nor did he look like he didn't believe me. "I've seen some of my relatives before too," my dad confessed. "I mean, after they died. I've seen some of my relatives too," he repeated. "I haven't seen Mom, though, but I dream about her all of the time. Mostly she is yelling at me."

Chuck and I laughed, knowing that was probably not a dream, but a visit. My mom and dad bickered constantly. There was love, but there were a lot of exhausting fights too.

I had joked with my mom that she was probably at the mall, and I do believe that she sensed I needed a Mom sighting and went there to help me, which it did. But often the sightings, dreams, and visits can be confusing.

Just a few months after my mom passed away, I was gifted with a visit from her where she took me grocery shopping. We both walked down aisle upon aisle, both pushing the same cart as I asked her questions about Heaven. "You couldn't take me to the Garden of Eden, but instead to a grocery store?" I asked her, a little bit peeved. She only laughed and I woke up. That was in 2006, and I can still see every single detail of that visit, from what she was wearing to what I was wearing. My mom was blind in life and grocery stores were over-stimulating for her, with the buzz of the fluorescent lights, the echoes of voices with the tall ceilings, and the many smells and various other noises. I took the visit as a way for my mom to show me that she didn't have her disability any longer and grocery stores weren't a bad thing anymore. I still would've preferred a beautiful garden, but the JCPenney encounter made up for it!

Betsy

"I hadn't gone to church since Ben died," Betsy, my elderly client, shared with me, "but I went last Sunday morning. As I was sitting in the pew that Ben and I always sat in I started to get weepy, when a young man came and sat down next to me."

Betsy took a tissue and wiped a tear. "He looked just like my Ben did when we first met. He simply touched my arm, looked me in the eyes, and said, 'You look awfully pretty today' and then got up and left. I was so stunned, I didn't even thank him, and then the first hymn played and it was the song that was at Ben's funeral, 'How Great Thou Art.' I looked everywhere for the stranger during the service and after, but the man was nowhere. Nowhere," Betsy repeated in disbelief. "Do you think that it was my Ben, Kristy?"

I smiled and nodded. "I do, Betsy. He looked healthy and young, didn't he?"

"Oh, yes. He looked very handsome. And he always told me that I looked pretty, even when I didn't look pretty," Betsy laughed. "I knew it was him. I feel him around me, but I also dream about him, and he is always young and without any pain. It is so reassuring."

Rita

Rita was mourning. Her only child, her daughter, Bonnie, had committed suicide, and it had been weeks since Rita slept a full night. Rita had tried to help Bonnie, but drugs and a bad group of friends had won over, and now death was Bonnie's ultimate reward and the worst curse for Rita. "At first I thought it was the lack of sleep," Rita shared. "It was three weeks to the day that Bonnie overdosed when I saw her standing in the doorway of my bedroom. She was wearing her favorite plaid shirt and jeans. Her hair was pulled back with a hair band and she had this sweet smile on her face. I got out of bed, or at least I thought I did, and stood in front of her. She gave me a hug, turned around, and walked down the hallway into a bright light and disappeared. I felt such a sense of peace after that. Oh, I still miss her, but that visit was … well, the most comforting gift that I could've received."

Ned

Ned's visitation with his wife happened almost a year to the date after she passed from a tragic car accident. "I hadn't received one sign, not one. I thought she was mad at me," Ned told me over the phone. "But the night before the one-year anniversary of Jodi's accident, I had fallen asleep in the recliner. It was a habitual thing even when Jodi was here. She would wake up in the middle of the night to use the bathroom or get a glass of water and shake me awake in the recliner so I could hop into bed. Well, I woke up to hearing my name called. Standing right in front of me was Jodi and she said, 'Isn't it time for you to go to bed?' But I heard it in my head. Her mouth never moved. She walked toward the bedroom and disappeared. I got up and followed her, but she wasn't anywhere. I'm an engineer, so it didn't make sense to me until my friend told me that it was a visit. Jodi showing that she was still watching over me."

Visits are a gift and it is very reassuring to know that our loved ones are still with us, but be patient as there is no time on the other side—what might be a year here may only feel like seconds there.

Chapter Nine

Music

The Other Side loves to share the message through music. You might wake up to a random song that you don't recognize, then read the lyrics only to find that it is more than likely a message. The Other Side may also send you music that creates a memory.

Allan's mom passed away just a few months before his first daughter, Hope, was born. Before her passing, she gave Allan and his wife the gift of a baby mobile with butterflies. After their baby was born, it became an almost nightly occurrence for him to wake up to hear the mobile playing its music over the baby monitor. As Hope got older, she would giggle and point toward the corner of the room, or look upwards and smile. Allan believed that his mom was cherishing being a grandma even from the Other Side.

After a long day at the office, Missy was irritated and driving home. She missed her mom so badly, especially on days like the one she had. Her mom had been her sounding board and counselor, but when her mom passed away from pancreatic cancer the year before, Missy felt like she had let her mom down. "Oh mom, I'm sorry. I wish you would give me a sign." As if on cue, the song on the pop radio station changed to a classic song by Anne Murray named "You Needed Me," a favorite of Missy's mom. Missy had to pull over and listen, crying the whole time. She had received her sign.

Music is the universal language, even into the Afterlife.

The Music Man

Charles Robinette was the oldest of two, growing up in Detroit during the Depression era. At a young age he showed signs of being a musical prodigy and his instrument of choice was the piano. A temperamental child, Charlie lent himself to becoming a temperamental man. Moody, yet musically brilliant, as he aged it became apparent that he bled music and his career was to be none other than that.

His mom would often tell the stories of Charlie waking up in the middle of the night screaming that he couldn't get the tunes out of his head. And both his daytime and nighttime became inundated with music.

His parents did give him piano lessons, but Charlie was naturally gifted, being able to play almost any instrument effortlessly, such as the xylophone, drums, and violin. Although he did read music, he could also play by ear.

As a student, Charlie was the musical director and band leader at McKenzie High School in Detroit, Michigan, and his real first job was playing the piano and touring on the road with the Ralph Martiree Orchestra, as the youngest member in the band.

Charlie was working at the Brass Rail Bar as the pianist while Mary Lou VanEtten was working as a bar maid. It was their love of jazz and big band music that was the catalyst for the love between them.

In 1961 Mary Lou and Charlie welcomed a baby boy, my husband. Labor was difficult for Mary Lou and she had to have an emergency c-section. She was weak and had lost a lot of blood, so as Mary Lou was still recovering from her surgery, Charlie named the baby after himself, Charles Edward Robinett, without his wife's permission. Charlie also lent out her collection of records to his buddies and members of his current band. Fifty years later Mary Lou still holds a grudge for this—the records more so than the naming of her son, since her prized collection was never returned.

It wasn't long after my husband, whom they nicknamed Robbie, was born that the marriage began to deteriorate, and although it would be another decade before Mary Lou and Charlie legally divorced, Robbie's grandparents, Charlie's parents, became his stability for most of his life. With Mary Lou being a single mom, although not legally, and Charlie busy with his music, Robbie's relationship with his father was vacant.

In the mid-60s Charlie worked as the orchestra leader at Detroit's famous Roostertail, a riverfront nightclub that was often visited by musical celebrities such as Tony Bennett, Paul

Anka, and Wayne Newton, many of which asked Charlie to join them on tour. Charlie rejected the offers as he didn't want to leave Detroit, yet he stayed in close contact with many of the musical artists that would become huge stars.

In the mid-70s Charlie also became a session musician for many rhythm and blues artists, including The Spinners. In the early 1970s Charles Robinette recorded several songs with The Spinners, playing the piano. Two of the songs are still frequently played today, "Games People Play" and "Rubberband Man."

During this time his son, Robbie, knew his father's successes, but wasn't at all interested. This was mostly because of the estranged and non-existent relationship, along with his father's excessive drinking, moodiness, and ego that alienated him from working relationships and a relationship with his son. Despite Robbie's grandmother's persistence that Robbie and Charlie have a father/son bond, Robbie's grudge kept his father at an emotional distance most all of his father's life. That was reiterated after Robbie had his own two daughters, Cora and Molly. Charlie would show up sporadically, and only on his terms, when it was convenient for him. It brought back painful memories for Robbie and he put his foot down. "You either show up when you say you will, and show up sober, or you don't show up at all." His dad's parents were wonderful to him, and he wanted nothing less than that for his own children. Eventually his dad just stopped showing up.

Charles Robinette, the man referred to as The Music Man, which is proudly displayed on his gravestone, passed

away from colon cancer in 1994. Robbie never truly recon-
ciled with him. That was until Robbie's fiftieth birthday, sev-
enteen years after his dad's death.

Not only did he and his father have different spellings
of their last name (everybody tries to put an *e* on the end of
Robinett, and his father thought Robinette looked better on
the marquee), I was first introduced to my now-husband as
Chuck while his whole family still calls him Robbie. Holidays can be confusing. But it was the night before Chuck's
fiftieth birthday when I was awakened by a man who looked
an awful lot like my husband.

"I want to give Robbie a birthday gift," the man in spirit
said, waking me from my sleep. "I want you to write him a
letter."

I wasn't quite sure what to make of it. I knew the difficult
relationship that they had. It was often that I heard Chuck
cuss out something his father did or didn't do, and I certainly
didn't want to ruin his special day. But the man, who was the
father-in-law I never met, didn't look like he was budging, so
I reluctantly got out of bed, put on a pink fuzzy robe, grabbed
my notebook, and quietly went to my office. He followed.

"Okay, now what?" I asked, with a taste of attitude.

"I want to first take you somewhere…"

In my mind's eye, Charlie walked me to a two-story building, with a stairway in the front, and in the back there were
large windows that overlooked water. He motioned for me to
sit on a barstool. In the corner there was a piano. I couldn't
make out much of the décor because it wasn't well lit, but it

wasn't the interior that he wanted to show me. It was more that it was a place where he was comfortable.

"Ready?"

I nodded and began to write, almost as if I was in a dream state.

> Happy Birthday, son. I love you. I wish that you had felt that. I tried at the end to tell you, but I guess I had upset you too much before.
>
> I didn't know how to be a dad or a papa and I did the worst I could at it. I'm sorry.
>
> Take care of your mom. She loves you. Tell the girls that I watch out for them even though they might not want me to. They are just beautiful.
>
> They used to call me Run Around Charlie. I hated that. I suppose I cheated mostly on you, though, Robbie.
>
> Be careful of your weight. It concerns me. I had my own issues and I never took care of it.
>
> I will make up for all of the wrongs. But you have to ask. You are a lot like me whether that makes you upset or not. We fester in the pain instead of allowing others to assist. Listen to the music. You'll know I am there.
>
> Remember, though, that in life and in the Afterlife, I love you. Happy Birthday.

I was very hesitant to give Chuck the letter that morning. It wasn't monumental. There were no lottery numbers or a treasure map, but I knew that his father meant well, and so I gave it to him.

Chuck and his father (even though I never met him in this life) have similar emotional reactions, that being non-reactive. He read the letter, folded it up, and put in his office. And nothing more was said. Until a few hours later when we were on our way to his birthday lunch. As we all chatted about this and that, "Rubberband Man" came on a top-40 station. Chuck and I looked at one another and laughed.

Since that time, either "Rubberband Man" or "Games People Play" come on the radio when any one of us—Chuck, his girls, and even sometimes myself—needs reassurance.

For example, Cora had just broken off a relationship and Molly convinced her to take a mini vacation and fly to Florida for a few days. After all, Cora's birthday was coming up, it was still frigid in Michigan, and some sun and sand would do them both good. They decided to stay at a small hotel near Tampa that had a good deal, only realizing later when they got there, the good deal was mainly because nothing much was around there. But they kept positive and took the time to lay by the pool, read a book, and talk. The quietness sometimes has a way of bringing up wounds, though, and Cora's mood turned melancholy until Molly and Cora realized the song that was being piped through the speakers by the pool. For the last few hours it had been pop and alternative music, but, well, this song was their own Papa's "Rubberband Man," and they both laughed and knew that he was saying to stop wallowing. They thanked their Papa Charlie for the nudge.

Just a year after the girl's Florida trip, Chuck and I were on our way to Molly's commencement from Michigan State University. She had worked hard to receive her degree in Forestry and Wildlife. It was about an hour drive from our home in Livonia, Michigan, to East Lansing, and we were meeting first at her apartment to celebrate and take photos with family before we headed to the auditorium. As we pulled into the parking lot of her complex, sure enough "Rubberband Man" came on the radio. Chuck just smiled and thanked his dad for keeping his promise to always be there with his girls.

Charlie continues to show himself through music at the most pivotal times. When Chuck had to have some medical tests done and we were concerned, "Games People Play" came on the radio in the waiting room. When my son, who isn't blood related at all to Charlie, was taken in for an emergency appendectomy, as I drove him to the hospital, "Rubberband Man" came just as we pulled into the drop-off lot. Two songs, not overly played, especially on FM radio, seem to be played just when we need the reassurance. We do believe it is The Music Man himself, Charles Robinette, who is busy caring for his family from the Other Side, even though he didn't quite have the hang of it here on Earth.

Chapter Ten

Other Signs from the Afterlife

Rainbows

The Other Side loves to share big and bright messages, and what better way than a rainbow. Many religions and spiritual thinkers believe that the rainbow is the bridge from this world to another.

Rainbows have been a symbol of promise and hope for years, most recognized in the Bible with Noah after the flood, and then again in pop culture with *The Wizard of Oz*. According to Native American legend, when a human dies, there is a Bridge that he or she must cross in order to enter Heaven. At the head of this Bridge awaits every animal that the individual had encountered during his or her lifetime. Based upon the legend, it is there that the animals decide who gets to cross the Rainbow Bridge and who doesn't.

Of course, there is a scientific explanation for the appearance of rainbows. However, that doesn't make them any less beautiful or miraculous to behold, and because of that, the Other Side likes to use the sign of the rainbow as a hello.

Somewhere Over the Rainbow

"How old are you?" I asked with a smile to the small and fragile-looking boy sitting in the wheelchair. I saw him looking at me over his long blond eyelashes.

The boy held up four fingers and sheepishly smiled back at me.

"Wow, I would've guessed that you were five years old." I grinned back at him.

The boy giggled and went back to playing with his handheld game system.

"I pray he makes it to five," his mom sighed. "My name is Kelly, by the way. This is Breegan," she shared, and gently stroked her son's light-colored hair

"I'm Kristy and this is Connor. I will send up a prayer too," I promised.

The brightly lit pre-surgery waiting room at Mott Children's Hospital in Ann Arbor, Michigan, was jam packed with children all waiting for various surgeries. I was holding my eleven-month-old, Connor, in my arms, who was starving for food and water, but hadn't been able to have anything after midnight. It was eleven o'clock in the morning and Connor's cleft palate surgery was delayed over two hours, which didn't help with anyone's orneriness. Yet, as I glanced around the room, many strangers were talking to other strangers, probably doing their best to try to relieve the anxiety of the unknown.

Kelly went on to tell me that her son, Breegan, was born with spine problems and they were hoping that the surgery he was waiting for, followed by intense physical therapy, would help him with at least some limited walking. I offered a reassuring smile. Connor's surgery wasn't routine and came with risks as all surgeries did, but it didn't seem as severe as what Breegan had to deal with. I noticed that Kelly didn't have anyone with her and I almost felt guilty. I had Connor's dad there, along with a hospital social worker, Cindy, whom I had befriended throughout the process of researching all that went into parenting a child born with a cleft palette, who was also mostly deaf.

Connor's dad was reading a magazine, so I got up and took a seat next to Breegan's mom and asked if she wanted to hold my hand—something that might sound weird unless you are ever in a hospital waiting to entrust your child's life to a staff of medical professionals. Cindy asked if she could take Connor and Breegan to the play room and we both nodded. So I held the stranger's hand, looked in her eyes, and told her that we both needed a time out. We both laughed, and then we prayed. For the remaining half hour we simply held hands until both of our sons were called, ironically at the very same time.

If you have experienced handing over your baby for major surgery, you know that it is as if a piece of your heart and soul is ripped apart from you as they wheel him/her into the operating room. It is the most heart wrenching and humbling experience. I kissed and hugged Connor, choking back the tears of fear. As they wheeled him down the long white corridor, I saw Kelly kiss and hold onto Breegan the same as I did to Connor, and then she began to softly sing "Over the Rainbow" in the most angelic voice ever. Breegan joined in and continued singing as he was wheeled away. I mustered a small smile for Kelly, offered her a hug, and went into the waiting room where I broke down.

It was several hours later when we were called in to hold Connor as he was crying for his mommy, and although I wasn't expecting all of the tubes and blood, I was grateful my child was alive and that he would heal.

Once settled into a room, the nurse came in and told Connor's dad and me that during our stay we were to take advantage of the massages, the coffee shop, the chapel, and the reading room—that we needed to have our own time out. I laughed at the choice of words, and leaving Connor in the capable and loving hands of his father, snuck away for a few minutes to go to the chapel. I found Breegan's mom stiffly sitting and staring ahead. The look on her face told me everything I needed to know.

"He isn't in any more pain," she said, through her sobs. "He's my angel forever. He's made it over the rainbow."

There wasn't anything I could say or do, except nod and hold her hand until a minister came in and took Breegan's mom from me.

That was fifteen years ago.

I had a different last name then and was working a different profession. And I never knew Breegan's mom's full name, nor did she know mine, but somehow she found me (or someone led her to me).

When Breegan came through, showing me how he looked fifteen years ago, and then showing me a nineteen-year-old version of himself, I smiled. Kelly didn't recognize me at first, nor did I recognize her, but Breegan knew, and when he told me to tell his mom that she wasn't taking enough time outs, and that he sent her rainbows, both of our eyes sparkled with tears.

Breegan didn't just come through to let his mom know that he was okay on the Other Side; he also offered a message that I asked his mom if I could share with all of you.

It's okay to fall apart. You don't have to put up an act or pretend to be strong. It's healthy to cry, as it helps shed and shake the sadness from your soul. Many times you hold so much on your shoulders that you just can't carry one more problem. Not one more. And most of the time nobody knows it. Your smile is so bright that they can't see the shadows around you. Cry. Shed. Release. Give yourself love. Always, always love.

No matter how much your soul aches, no matter your problems, make sure to take a time out.

After Breegan's passing, Kelly said she decided to get a tattoo of a rainbow on her back with Breegan's name in it. Without knowing that, Breegan gave her one last message and that was to always, always remember to look for the rainbows in her own life, because he was there with her every step of the way.

Numbers

Numbers are part of our everyday life; they are everywhere, and our loved ones can easily utilize this sign as a means to show us they are around. It might be a sequence of numbers that makes sense, or just a sequence of numbers that continue to reoccur, such as 1-1-1 or 1-2-3. Repetitive numbers such as 111, 222, 333, etc., or numbers that are connected to you or your loved one through a birthdate, a favorite number, anniversary date, etc., are not random or coincidental at all, but a way for your loved ones on the Other Side to try to connect with you. My birthdate is 11-13, and I will often look at the clock and see my birthdate numbers; I know that someone is saying hello from the other side.

444

Ryan was just one of the many firefighters that perished during the terrorist attack in New York City on September 11, 2001; he left behind four young kids and a grieving wife.

Kristen and Ryan had a special connection that many envied. They were high school sweethearts and although most high school relationships fizzle out, Kristen and Ryan weren't just lovers, they were best friends. Both were very supportive of one another's careers and were equal parents to their four girls.

Ryan came from a family of firefighters and it wasn't any surprise when he announced his career intentions. Any spouse of a first responder worries when they walk out the door, but Kristen believed in Ryan and trusted that he would make the smart and right decisions on duty and off. When Kristen received word of the attack, knowing that Ryan was on shift during that time, she knew that he was gone. "It was as if a limb was cut from me almost instantly," she explained to me. "Even though friends and family thought I was being pessimistic because we hadn't any official acknowledgement, I knew."

It was almost immediately that Kristen began receiving signs from Ryan. One of his favorite scents was vanilla. "He was always coming home with different vanilla candles. He'd go to the grocery store and bring home a vanilla candle. It became a running joke that I knew what the anniversary gift would be—a vanilla candle.

"It was that first night when I smelled a vanilla candle burning and got up to see if my mom had lit one and forgotten, but nothing was lit, yet the smell was so strong and I realized that was Ryan's way of telling me that he was okay. I told him that it was okay to go into the light and to cross. We have a strong Catholic faith."

The sightings of the triple fours began about a week later. Kristen told me that Ryan's badge number had a series of fours in it, his birthday was April 4, they had four girls, and four was his favorite number.

"Some might've thought it was a coincidence, but the amount of triple fours I saw, in the way that I saw them, was uncanny. From my mileage, to receipt numbers, license plates, and even the time of day. Anytime I became sad or started to grieve, there were the fours again, and I knew it was Ryan's way of telling me that he was there and to toughen up. It was comforting to know that he was around."

Four years after Ryan was killed, again not a coincidence on the time, Kristen remarried. "I knew that he was sent from Ryan when his license plate was a series of fours and he showed up sixteen minutes early, at 4:44."

Hearing

You might wake up in the middle of the night because you hear your name called, and think it was a dream, but more than likely it was a loved one on the Other Side just getting your attention for a Heaven hello.

Thoughts

That thought that you should call a friend you haven't heard from in a long time and then the phone rings is most likely a loved one on the Other Side trying to help bring some happiness and joy to you. There could also be a connection between the other person, you, and the loved one on the Other Side. Or you might just be going about your day and all of the sudden think of that person who passed away; that is them coming through with a hello.

Buzzing

Because our loved ones on the Other Side are made up of energy, they can disrupt our senses. Much like when you're flying in an airplane, when they are around us you might feel a vibration through the body or your ears may buzz or feel plugged.

Smells

Our loved ones love to send us familiar smells that elicit a memory of them. It can vary from the cigarettes that your grandpa used to smoke to the cookies that your mom used to bake.

Tastes

As with smells, spirit sends you tastes. You might just be sitting on the couch when you all of the sudden taste the spaghetti sauce your dad used to make.

Temperature Changes

Many have reported temperature changes, both cold and hot, when interactions with passed loves ones occur.

You will find ways to intentionally connect with loved ones on the Other Side in the Appendix under "Making the Connection With the Other Side."

Chapter Eleven

To Hell With It

Even though the majority of the spirits who visit me share lovely messages of their Afterlife, once in a while there are the tortured souls who also reach out to me, and sometimes those spirits can be angry and upset.

Forever Imprisoned

My entire life has revolved around the paranormal, the Afterlife, and the in-between life. If it didn't find me, I sought it. Lunch hours were frequently taken at the local historical cemetery where I would have peaceful conversations with those who had crossed over, and ghosts-in-waiting. Not once during my excursions did I stomp and storm about, force them to show themselves, demand they make lights flicker on my meters, or encourage that they move a toy. Well, it did (and still does) help that I am a medium and can see, sense, hear, and communicate with those on the Other Side. Just like many people, I have watched my fair share of paranormal shows. Some I love, some I tolerate, and then there are some that I just shake my head at in total disgust. If you have attended any of the ghost tours, ghost hunts, or overnights that I have hosted, you know the first thing I say is that ghost hunting is as exciting as watching paint dry. And the next thing I say is to respect the spirits and ghosts, as we live as one, under a different sky, a different paradigm, but still as one. So yelling and screaming at them in their home, or requesting them to do circus tricks that the family dog would more than likely give some choice words about if he could…well, it just doesn't cut it. It is disrespectful. Even snapping zillions of photographs, as if you are the paranormal paparazzi, is ridiculous.

Recently I have found so-called haunted locations denoting on their contracts that it will not be allowed for anyone in a group to cross over a spirit. *That they like their ghosts.* I wonder if they would feel the same way if the tables were turned and they missed the last train to Heaven. How they would feel being kept hostage? It is wise to approach paranormal situations as if the person is standing in front of you. Would you tell that person, "Sorry, I like the money that I am making off of you; therefore you aren't allowed to leave to be with your family"? Although I have come into contact with some soulless people in my lifetime, I doubt that the majority would have the guts to say that. So just because we cannot see these beings, why do so many feel that they have a stake in keeping them hostage? They don't, and shouldn't, and for those that do, just know that there may be a lovely karmic situation for you when you pass.

With Light Comes Dark

I was quite young when my dad took me to a local Presbyterian church to listen to a minister who proclaimed to travel to third-world countries and do exorcisms on the possessed. My dad wanted to record the program, just as many others were doing, but about five minutes into the program, the minister stopped and was horrified. "We must pray. I forgot to pray!" he proclaimed, visibly shaken. "We must protect ourselves when dealing with the darkness and ask that the recordings work." And so we prayed and he continued his lengthy lecture that included film of the horrific exorcisms that he conducted. When we returned home, my dad rewound the tape and hit play, but for the first five minutes all we heard were screams of horror, growls, and indescribable voices until we heard "amen" and the lecture continued without a problem. There was no explanation. We later asked others who had recorded the program and they all had the same horrific noises on tape. Did this prove that there was a Hell filled with wicked punishment and torture? To some, including my dad, it did.

In 2005 I was part of a popular online radio show where I interviewed an array of guests with topics in the paranormal, metaphysical, and the supernatural. I received a query to interview a gentleman on his near-death experience. I was interested and so we agreed on the date. He informed me that he officially flatlined and died for almost ten minutes after his appendix ruptured.

"Did you see a light, like many people who've encountered a near death?" I asked him.

"I saw nothing, Kristy," he replied. "The only thing I saw was darkness. There is no Afterlife. There is no Heaven. There is no Hell. There is nothing."

I was surprised and taken aback. We were three minutes into a sixty-minute interview and the last thing that I wanted to do was create a theological debate.

"I was a Presbyterian before and now I'm an atheist. I've decided to not give my money to something that doesn't even exist, to a farce. Religion, that is."

"So you don't believe you were brought back to complete some special mission or share a message?" I asked with the hopes that maybe he wasn't sharing everything.

"No, my message is to keep your bank account intact and to stop fronting money for huge and expensive cathedrals."

In situations like this there just wasn't any right thing to say. I simply thanked him for his story, his point of view, and let him go. For the remainder of the time I took calls from the listeners, who had a whole lot to say.

I was stunned to see that same man on my schedule four years later. To say that I was nervous was an understatement, but I kept an open mind as I greeted him at my office door and offered him a chair. I saw his wife standing in back of him in spirit. A light pink light shone behind her and she smiled.

"Your wife is standing in back of you, Zed. She says that you did everything to save her, but it was her time."

Zed bowed his head and sobbed. "Is she really there, Kristy? You aren't just saying that?"

"I promise, I am not just saying that."

Zed looked up at me, the corners of his eyes wrinkled. "I think I'm being punished. I think that when I died I experienced Hell and when I came back, I experienced more of the same. Nothing went my way afterward. Terry left me, you know?"

"She still calls herself your wife, though, so I don't think she gave up on you, but you on her. That darkness that you described…"

Zed interrupted me before I could finish. "That darkness that I saw when I died, well, I think it was the darkness that was in my heart. If I just took off my closed-minded glasses then maybe I would have seen something more, but that was my Hell and I made that Hell my reality. It still is."

Previous to Zed's near-death experience, he had lost his business, his dad to cancer, and most everything that he thought equated to what his identity was, and then the only person that loved him for who he was no matter what.

"You asked me years ago if I thought there was a message that I was supposed to share."

I quietly nodded, still glancing over at Terry, who put her hand on his left shoulder.

"I think I missed that message. I think the message was that Hell absolutely exists. It exists within each one of us, but so does Heaven. It isn't a place, Kristy, it's an existence. It is what we make it. It is our now. It is our Afterlife too. I don't want this darkness anymore, Kristy."

Zed passed away last year. His son sent me his obituary with a note saying that his dad had denounced atheism, and although he wasn't a regular churchgoer, Zed learned to believe again.

In my many years of doing sessions, I never once had anyone come through and tell me that they were in Hell and that they needed my help. But does that mean that there isn't a Hell? No, it just means that either they don't have my number or me theirs. Or maybe in Hell they aren't allowed to make connections.

Many believe that once we receive our life review when we cross, we receive forgiveness and are given our choir robes and our room key. That, however, has not been how those on the Other Side have explained it to me, and there have been thousands and thousands who tell me what the Afterlife entails. They aren't all exact; just as our birth stories are different, our death stories are different, and so is our Afterlife story.

The Invitation

"Can I be specific with who I want to talk to, Kristy?" Deena, the sixty-something mother of three, grandmother of seven, asked me.

"Invite in who you want to speak with, but there are no guarantees, unfortunately," I explained. "It seems that the people who come through aren't necessarily the ones we think will come through, but the ones that need to come through. Maybe at the time we don't realize it, but in the end it is." I closed my eyes, took a deep breath, said a small prayer, and asked for clear and concise messages.

Deena's mom, dad, and both sets of grandparents came through with messages, and then I saw a tall man with thinning dark brown hair and a mustache standing at the end of what looked like a long tunnel. He avoided looking at me, his head hanging down, but he stood there nonetheless. "Do you have a message for Deena?" I telepathically asked him. He held up his hand in a gesture that asked to give him a moment.

"Who is it, Kristy?" Deena puzzled.

"A man who feels a lot of remorse and is afraid to completely come through to me," I replied and went on to describe him. "I think his name is Warren or Walden."

Dena gasped and shook her head as if trying to swat a wasp out of her hair.

Alarmed, I asked the man for a quick message and saw that he was now sobbing. "Tell Dee that I am so very sorry. I'm paying for what I did and am still learning and growing. Ask her to tell my brother Will that I am sorry too." He turned around and the tunnel he was in just disappeared. Her mom, and her dad named Will, continued to stand in back of her. I checked Will's expression and he looked horrified; his hands were on his daughter's shoulders, as if trying to steady her, even in spirit.

"That person was my dad's brother. He molested me when I was nine years old. I wasn't his first either. My dad and his family were in denial, and nobody ever told my mom about Uncle Warren's past. If she had known at the time, she would have never left me with him. I told my mom and dad what happened, but not until after Uncle Warren died, three years later. He committed suicide and he included a note that confessed everything, asking forgiveness."

I didn't know what to say. My sessions were to bring peace, not pain. I was dumbfounded.

"Is he in Heaven? Or did we just get a visit from Hell?" Dee's questions seemed to echo. Why didn't Warren see Will?

I never believed I had all the answers. With each session, I learn more and more about the Afterlife. I sat there for a moment, stunned, feeling absolutely horrible for bringing the connection through and for what Deena had endured. "He wanted you to tell your dad that he was sorry. So he must not know that he has passed away."

"Doesn't everybody who passes away meet for a reunion?" Deena inquired. "Good and bad?"

It was a good question and one that I had been asked many times. Why couldn't Warren see Will, or at least know that he had died? So I asked the only person who could answer that for me at that moment—Deena's dad, Will.

Will explained to us that he was not reunited with his brother, nor would he want that reunion. "Heaven is what we want from it. Where we want it to be and we are with the people we want to be with. What you call Hell, well," Will drawled, "you don't get those choices or interactions. I get to visit with my family in Heaven and on Earth; in the darker plane, you didn't get an ultimate pass."

Deena leaned into me, her brow furled in thought. "So if those in Hell don't get passes, how did he come visit us?"

I looked again to Will for help. "I didn't say that there were never passes, just not endless passes. Those from Hell can visit for two reasons—to give peace and to give pain; it is ultimately our faith that decides which one we choose."

"Can those in Hell ever move to Heaven?" Deena asked.

Will's eyes narrowed and answered with a simple no.

Deena decided to use the visit from her uncle as a means to find peace. Not peace with him, per say, but according to her, she'd kept the molestation like a souvenir instead of throwing it away. She'd allowed it to become her personal Hell and, after so many decades, she was done with it.

This Is Hell

So is ghost hunting entertainment or really something more serious? And can it prove that Heaven and/or Hell exists? I've had my share of experiences, but in 2012 I was offered the opportunity to give paranormal tours to a group of ghost seekers at the old historic Jackson Prison (1837–1935) in Jackson, Michigan. Now called Armory Arts Village, what once held inmates in four tiers of prison cells is now a beautiful artist community with apartments, condominiums, and art studios. Still intact is the prison's solitary confinement area and the old tunnels where unimaginable things happened to the prisoners because it was "out of sight." I am cautious where I take the public, as I have gone toe-to-toe with a demon and survived (obviously), but it is nothing that I would ever recommend to a novice or even an expert investigator. I didn't feel awful about Michigan's First State Prison. It felt like a relatively safe place, and I was assured by tenants that although there was so much activity, it had never been too negative. "Too" being the operative word.

One tour started off uneventful, until the City of Jackson lost power after a drunk driver ran into a transformer. Most of the group left after that (whether tired or scared...we may never know), and we were left with a core group of investigators interested in venturing down into the tunnel once more. As we sat crouched and waiting, we all began to feel as if we were the ones hunted. The energy shifted into something that felt almost mocking. With our instruments lighting up and a toy car being moved with ethereal hands, we heard whispers. To break up the tension, we decided on a sing-along, which entertained both the group and the ghosts.

At one point we received a message from a man who wanted to cross over. He was done being stuck. He was done hiding from his judgment, for possibly he had already served his time and knew it. So I did what any good investigator should do—I asked the group to help me cross him over. The energy shifted; it lifted. Many in the group sniffled. I cried. I didn't cry because I was afraid that the next group I brought in might be ghost-less; I cried because we had helped reunite this spirit with his family and friends after so much time.

He may have never received that opportunity if it wasn't for us. Not once did I think of just walking away from him. Call me a sucker, or a helper, or even a healer, I would refer to the whole group as ghost Samaritans. And maybe that is why the power went out. And maybe that is why we decided to venture down there instead of someone's apartment, which was on the itinerary. There is nothing random in life, there is always a reason.

When we left, I didn't feel as if I had given the group an entertaining time. I think some may have left thinking back to the beginning of the lecture and agreeing that ghost hunting was indeed much like watching paint dry and they would probably never do it again. While I think others felt the adrenaline of helping, not just hunting.

It was the very last paranormal tour that I held at the old Michigan prison that put an exclamation mark on the end of a sentence. Rumors were that the tours were stirring up paranormal activity for the residents and they asked that no more be scheduled, so it was our last hoorah.

A group went into the tunnels where we had witnessed odd white and green lights shining, whispers, and even gentle touches. As we went to change rooms, four of us stayed crouched near the end of the tunnel where we heard a growl and a hissing noise. Instead of turning around and going toe-to-toe with whatever entity was upset, we ran. This is a regret I still have today, but then it is easier to say now than in that situation.

We then headed down into solitary confinement where Hannibal the Bear, a man with a bad temper, had spent more than four years of his life and was a legendary ghost who haunted the area. Armed with a spirit box that uses radio frequencies to give ghosts or spirits a voice, along with recorders and other paranormal equipment, about ten of us sat down on the dirt floor and tried to make contact. Immediately on the spirit box we heard a growl, similar to the one we had heard in the tunnels, and then a man's voice came through, answering our questions clearly.

"I'm not a good person. I've killed many. Mostly children."

When we asked him what year it occurred, he replied that it was in 1866. And when we asked him where he was, he replied ominously, "This is Hell."

In Between

The Catholic catechism clearly spells out that there is a Purgatory where you can find purification of the soul after death: "All who die in God's grace and friendship, but still imperfectly purified, are indeed assured of their eternal salvation; but after death they undergo purification, so as to achieve the holiness necessary to enter the joy of Heaven. The Church gives the name Purgatory to this final purification of the elect, which is entirely different from the punishment of the damned."

Purgatory, or Limbo as some call it, has been shown to me differently than how many religions teach it to be. As Will said to his daughter Deena, there is no way to elevate a soul by praying for them or that soul doing good works in order to win their way into a heavenly realm. It isn't work that someone else does for them, but work they have to do for themselves. Purgatory and Limbo are often self-made, self-created; a waiting room of sorts for the soul to step across and allow the Soul Review and then the final journey. Many have fears that what they've done on Earth will send them to a fire-and-brimstone place, so the waiting room for them is better than that. And so they wait. Many of those waiters are what are called ghosts, and the souls of the ghosts wander aimlessly.

The Ohio State Reformatory (or Mansfield Reformatory) in Mansfield, Ohio—seen on popular paranormal shows such as *Ghost Adventures*, *Ghost Hunters Academy*, and *My Ghost Story*—has been noted as one of the top haunted locations in the world. It has been utilized for many movie and music videos, most notoriously for the movie *Shawshank Redemption*. On Sunday, August 19, 2013, twenty-nine of us investigated the historical location.

The Ohio State Reformatory was built by Freemasons in 1886 and was designed to rehabilitate first-time offenders. The architecture was (and still is) spectacular, originally modeled to resemble a castle, and so it was thought that this would be a positive step for prison reform. Unfortunately, conditions rapidly deteriorated and this prison was left with a haunting legacy of abuse, inhumane torture, many murders, and secrets that are still contained within the walls. Civil Rights activists lobbied successfully to shut the prison down in 1990 because the prisoners resided with rats, bugs, bats, moldy and decaying food, and disease. Violence was an everyday occurrence, as was bloodshed. Five years later, in 1995, the Mansfield Reformatory Preservation Society opened the prison for ghost hunts.

Considered to have the largest freestanding steel cell block in the world, the prison's six levels is massive. Even while being built, deaths occurred with workmen falling off scaffolding. Also used as a tuberculosis overflow area, sick civilians were purposefully housed in the hospital near the prisoners with the hopes of thinning the over-crowded population.

Many of the television shows note hot spots for paranormal activity, including the Warden's quarters where the Warden's wife was shot when she apparently reached for something in her closet. It is said that the smell of her perfume can be detected. The Hole, solitary confinement, and the Infirmary were also noted as active spots. But there are other areas, miles and miles, to explore. And as I always say, ghosts don't necessarily have to be stuck in one area—they can move around. Ghosts are different than spirits. Spirits are those that cross over but come back to visit, while ghosts are those who decide not to or cannot cross over for a variety of reasons.

Communication is different for me as a medium, but I also believe it is different for those doing the investigations. Spirits don't typically haunt—they visit. On that Sunday we went in search of what lurked within the stone walls of Mansfield Reformatory. In the dark.

The investigation began at 8 p.m. and would last until 5 a.m., where we had free reign of 95 percent of the building. Hallways, tunnels, and hundreds and hundreds of stairs were confusing but exciting, as with every turn and every floor, we explored the tiered building. The floors were dusty, fireplaces were broken, windows cracked, and it was home to many animals—living and dead. But no matter, Mansfield showed off her glory and shined even through the grime.

I see ghosts. And spirits. But when I do investigations I don't want to be the center of attention, I want participants to experience what they experience without me pointing and narrating. I do share. And I do get scared, which to some may seem odd, but I have not lost the human innocence of the abnormality of seeing, hearing, feeling, and communicating with what most people can't and don't want to see, hear, feel, and communicate with. Mansfield didn't disappoint. I was grabbed, touched, growled at, cried to, and spoken to. My biggest issue, though, wasn't of the paranormal kind. It was bats.

We had a group of about ten people going into a room down a long and narrow corridor when I heard the warning sign. I yelled, "Bats! Move—go, go, go." The group, confused and only hearing "go, go, go," began to slowly walk back toward the entrance when I demanded they turn off their flashlights and go faster. It wasn't until the screeching and the wing-flapping over our heads that they realized it wasn't a ghost, or anything demonic, but living (I think) bats. Chuck was at the end of the corridor walking away from us when I yelled out "bat" and he turned around and was smacked in the face with the fuzzy black being. I am not sure I have laughed that hard in a long time.

The night continued with bats pestering me (karma?). So between one of the participants making bat noises to drive me, well, batty, and flapping his baseball hat to make bat noises in my ear (remember—we were in the dark), and the real bats dive-bombing me, I hit the deck a few times and banged up my knee. My screams were becoming too frequent, so I kept my hand over my mouth and my eyes closed as I walked through one of the cells as everybody looked and laughed on, but I didn't want to keep them from the real reason we were there—the experience.

Cameras malfunctioned, video cameras came on by themselves or wouldn't turn on, paranormal equipment refused to work, and as we tried to make heads or tales of it all, the 95 percent full moon cascaded light within windows, until an orange fog blanketed the prison—and only the prison. We watched it inch in from the Warden's home and block the moon, which was the only light we had other than our flashlights (this was one reason why we were having bat issues—LED lights confuse the creatures' senses). At one point I felt like sitting down and sobbing, and that sad energy continued with me two days later.

Although there'd been hardcore prisoners housed there, many of the prisoners were petty thieves. The prison had encountered thousands of deaths, and held the souls of the many who still haven't crossed over, making this a favorite location for ghost hunters.

In the middle of the investigation, a group of us made our way to what had been the infirmary and had communication with a man named William and another named Russ. Russ said he was in his seventies and he was ready to be with his family. He said that he had not murdered anybody, but that he stole money and because of his religion he felt as if wasn't deserving of Heaven. Several us sat in the then-hospital and crossed him and William over. There was a dog that looked like a spaniel or small shepherd who ran around the Warden's hallway and we did in fact smell rose perfume, which had become almost legend for when the Warden's wife was around. Just as soon as we smelled it, it would disappear.

I could barely sleep when we returned to the hotel at five in the morning, thinking that maybe my mission at the prison wasn't completed and wondering when I could return to possibly find keys that could unlock more lost souls and assist them in finding final freedom. I've always felt that was the true reason for paranormal investigations. Not treating the ghosts like caged animals at the zoo where we are the jail keepers, but to almost be the counselor and release them, yet they have to do the work. They have to make the full commitment to cross over.

After returning home, my family began to encounter some interesting activity. It started with every single one of our battery-operated clocks stopping, almost simultaneously on 4:35. Then there was the smell of cigar smoke and bad body odor followed by the shadows. When my teenagers told me that they were getting scared, and they had seen and heard a lot in their lifetime because of my work, I knew that Chuck and I had brought home a hitchhiker from the prison, so I sat down to see if I could figure out who it was.

"Okay, who are you?" I said out loud and feeling like a nut. "Come out, come out, wherever you are! Hide-and-seek is over."

The shadow that was frightening my kids so much manifested into a man, his eyes darting back and forth. I looked around to make sure that the producers of *Supernatural* weren't hiding in my linen closet with a camera.

"So what's your story?" I demanded. "And tell it quick, because I don't have time for games. You've scared my kids. I am exhausted, and to be honest, I'm not a nice person when I am exhausted."

For the next twenty minutes, the ghost went on to tell me his life, and his death story. His name was Fred and he said that he had served time in Mansfield in the late 1800s. "I attempted to shoot a man, Ma'am, but I was never a good shot, and I missed." Fred had a bit of a southern drawl about him and didn't have the energy of a hardnosed criminal. He shared that when he came home for lunch he found his wife with another man and in a moment of fury, he took out a gun and shot the other man. Well, attempted to. He ran, but was found the next day hiding underneath the porch of his friend's home. A year after his conviction, he hanged himself. "Even if I got out of prison, I had nowhere to go and no one to go home to. I was always slow. Only good for this and that tasks. My dad told me that I wasn't a real man and my mom never stuck up for me. So nobody even met me after I died."

I wanted to be upset with Frank, but I felt sorry for him more than anything. "And you followed me home because?"

"I saw you help those other men. You were kind and I thought maybe you could help me too. I'm ready to meet my judgment, Ma'am, whatever that might entail. I've been imprisoned for a long time."

"Years," I muttered. "Over a hundred years. That itself had to be Hell. I can help bring through the light for you, but you must do the work of walking to it and walking through it. Can you do that?"

Frank nodded. His energy shifted and it felt as if years of sludge was being exfoliated off of him. "What will happen once I cross into the light?" Frank hesitantly asked.

"You will have what is called a Life or Soul Review, where you will experience the emotions, effects, and experiences that your actions caused others, and yourself," I added. I could sense the fear around Frank again. "Look, Frank, nobody is a saint. We were destined to have peace in this life, and peace in the Afterlife. The choice is ultimately up to you. Do you choose to feed the positive, or to feed the negative? Your choices are pretty limited at this point."

Frank nodded in agreement.

I closed my eyes, said a prayer, and invited in my angels and guides to help me. "I, along with my angels and Spirit Guides, will help light a pathway for you. You are going to see a bright white staircase that sprawls up to the ceiling and beyond. Do you see that?"

Frank nodded his head yes.

"And step by step, I want you to climb those steps up. With each step you feel more confident in your crossing over.

And as you climb higher, you will see figures standing at the top to help you walk through the doorway to the Other Side."

I could see three figures standing at the top of the lit stairwell. Two were angelic figures and the other was a female. Maybe his mom or grandmother. It wasn't time for me to make a connection, but instead to help him cross over. As Frank climbed, he began to weep, but with each step it was as if he were shedding his burdens and becoming lighter until he was at the top of the staircase, encased in a bright light. He hugged the woman that I saw meet him and the four of them walked through a doorway, then the staircase disappeared.

I opened my eyes and closed them again, trying to sense if I could feel anything, but the space felt empty.

It was a few months after Frank's crossing that I woke up to a man nudging my shoulder. I opened my eyes, surprised to see none other than Frank standing there. He was sheathed in a brilliant white light that glowed. And like a first-grader who got a gold star on his report card, he whispered, "I'm in Heaven. I made it to Heaven! Thank you!" Frank simply dissipated and I rubbed my eyes to make sure I wasn't dreaming. I picked up my cell phone to check the time, and the numbers glared back at me—4:35 a.m.

"Good job, Frank," I whispered. I set my cell phone back down on my nightstand and went back to sleep.

Phil

Sometimes I forget what normal is. No matter where I go, where I am, or who I am with, I see (and most of the time communicate with) those who have physically died. I try to bubble myself off with a white light, a shield if you will, so that contact is limited and I am not looking like a lunatic talking to what most people would only see as air, but what I see as energy or a spirit. Sometimes the energy/spirit is strong-willed and stubborn and wants that contact and will attempt to get my attention no matter what. And when they can see that I can see, the avoidance doesn't just feel rude, it feels sad. How many people can actually see and communicate? Probably more than we realize, but they ignore or busy themselves. How many can give the stories from the Other Side to their loved ones? I can and I have taken on the role of being that messenger.

What should've been a simple hour of time waiting for my son to get a haircut ended up in story time with Phil.

Phil had committed suicide after a painful diagnosis that numbered his life span, and even though he was raised Catholic and had faith, he didn't feel as if he could hold on anymore. This was his story he asked me to share with his family, and the girl who was cutting my son's hair—his daughter.

A man who was frail in body, dying, and sad in heart showed me his spirit as he was before he passed away. He said that he needed to say he was sorry for hurting everybody and causing the difficulties that he did, especially the way that he ended his life. He hadn't wanted anybody to find him that way, but he didn't know any other way. He was scared of dying, but he was more scared of living and he didn't want to burden anybody anymore.

He showed me a darkened room. He sat on the edge of the bed, holding the gun in his hand. He didn't show me the death (most do), but instead showed me the tension beforehand and then the loud noise that took his physical life. Over and done. *What a quick second*, he thought, that quick second that ended his life and changed so many.

He showed himself crying beforehand, taking a deep breath, and then crying in spirit afterward—surprised by his own actions. He showed that he was grounded, not able to cross over for some time. His Purgatory was having to watch the anguish that his actions caused his kids and other loved ones. The shame he felt was worse than a physical death, he explained, but he said that he didn't have the fight in him. He continued to defend his actions by saying that over and over.

He said he could see the light, but that he was too exhausted to meet the angels, not even halfway, so he sat there wondering if he had done the right thing. They called to him. He cried. He saw his loved ones standing there, but felt as if he might not be good enough to be with them, or that his judgment might not be one he wanted to face and would put him in a worse place. Could it be possible that he had made a huge error? He said he asked himself that over and over again.

What seemed like months, but was only a week, he finally took the hike to the light. He said that his love, his wife, was there and when he saw her, he sobbed in her arms. And then it was time for him to be counseled, he explained. I asked him if that was like judgment and he nodded, but said it was judgment done with love and not with fire and brimstone.

After what I call Angel Boot Camp counseling, Phil showed himself in a good place with his loved ones and his wife. He was in a small, simple home that sat on a crystal blue lake. He had on a flannel shirt and his spirit looked healthy and happy. He said that he tried to visit his family, but that everybody on this side was just so stressed that his visits instead induced nightmares of his closed casket and weren't true visits.

"Miss, you see me. Please send my love and the message that I am proud of everybody. Please tell all the kids that they need to take care of themselves and to please forgive me. Mom and I love them so much."

He then shared a message that I thought was the deepest of all, and advice I thought we all needed.

"Enjoy the family. Enjoy life. Enjoy the simple things. Enjoy one another. I am okay."

I rarely go up to strangers and offer messages, but he insisted that I put my magazine down and write a letter to his daughter. I wrapped the cash tip for Connor's haircut inside the letter and handed it to her on our way out. Confused with what I gave her, the hairdresser caught up to me, tears streaming down her face, before I even closed my car door.

"You have no idea how much this means to me," she said, embracing me. "How can I repay you?"

"Forgive your dad and do as he says," I said and smiled.

We all hold on to anger, even with those who aren't with us physically. They know. They feel. They sense. They see. And they want to be a part of your life, but it is that anger that can cause fuzz and a bad connection on the telephone line to the Other Side. It can, however, be repaired with some soul searching, but let me tell you that once it is repaired, the phone will keep ringing. And that is a good thing.

My experiences with those on the Other Side who have committed suicide have been as different as each individual's life. Some have regrets, and some don't. Some aren't in the best place on the Other Side, although I wouldn't exactly define it as Hell, and others transition just fine, and are at peace and are happy with their decision. There is, however, no escape from our problems on this side or the next.

Marcia

Marcia came to me for a session. About sixty years of age, her short brown hair and glasses made her look like an elementary teacher. There was a softness about her energy that exuded a matriarch-like characteristic. It was her husband in spirit who decided to come through for her.

Marcia's husband looked a bit like Clint Eastwood and he took that as a compliment as I shared his physical attributes to his wife, mostly for validation. He said his name was Ray and showed me a sun ray to help clarify.

"He says that you are angry with him, Marcia. Really, really angry at him."

Marcia wiped her tears, but just sat staring at me.

"I killed myself," Ray confessed. "I killed myself," he repeated, and started to sob. And then he showed me the details.

"He says that he took a belt and went to the local park and hung himself," I sympathetically said, tears forming in my own eyes as I relayed his passing.

Marcia nodded and just stared at me with her big brown eyes.

"Tell her that I am sorry. It had nothing to do with her or the kids. Oh boy, I love those kids. I just felt useless. I had to retire because of my back and I felt useless."

"Tell her I am with the kids, especially Sammy. I promised him the summer before I died that I would take him fishing. I know that he hasn't fished since. Tell Marcia that I want him to fish and that I will be with him when he does."

I shared what he told me.

"Kristy, is he in Hell? We were both raised Catholic and that..." Marcia gulped and looked down, awaiting my answer.

I looked over at Ray. He shook his head no at me.

"He didn't go straight to Heaven, he says. He had a lot of depression to work on, along with a lot of unresolved issues with his dad. He had to get, well, the only way that I can explain it is like counseling. Once he got to a better place within his spirit and his soul, he could move on. But he's now in a better place."

Marcia's earlier tears turned to sobs of relief.

"I was supposed to take her to Hawaii for our thirtieth anniversary," Ray said, his energy emitting sadness. "I still want her to go. I know that Hawaii has many rainbows, but she will know the rainbow that I send her. I have been sending her them here, too, but she isn't paying attention. Tell her to watch for the rainbow."

Six months later I received a phone call from Marcia. "Kristy, you won't believe it. Although I didn't want to go to Hawaii because I felt like it was wrong to celebrate something that was no longer there, the whole time I felt Ray's presence. And the rainbow he mentioned, just as I got off of the plane. It was a triple rainbow. A triple rainbow! His favorite number was three and he was born in March. I had been doubting all the signs, and now, well, I believe. I still miss him, but I have my rainbows."

Hope for the Hopeless

"I'm just not going to do any more radio gigs," I whined to my friend on the phone.

I could hear her giggle on the other end, which only frustrated me more.

I was serious. I loved doing radio, but that particular morning the reviews on the station's Facebook page had been exceptionally harsh.

"I would love for the naysayers to *attempt* to read energy hundreds of miles away, connect to their past loved ones and guides in just a few seconds, and formulate positive advice. It is a bit like a dentist having several people with their mouths open and the dentist standing more than a hundred feet away with a microscope and making a diagnosis. It isn't easy, but I love the challenge and I love talking to people," I sighed, and then noticed that Kay hadn't responded at all. "Kay, are you even listening to me?"

"Uh huh. Dentist. Microscope. Energy."

"Grr," I growled and rolled my eyes, clicking off my computer.

Kay had heard me complain and whine for years. If I had a client who was exceptionally difficult, I cried to her. If I had a client who touched me to tears, I cried to her. I never gave away privileged information from the sessions—I believe in confidentiality—but she was my sounding board and for that I was eternally grateful.

Kay became my friend after being one of my clients herself. I was mentored from the beginning of doing sessions to not get too close to my clients, and to not befriend them, but there are some rules that I think are made for breaking and this was one of them. "But I don't like anybody thinking less of me, you know?" I continued whining.

"Kristy, you are in a business that will always be scrutinized. I know that your nature isn't to have armor on, but in situations like this, you either let it roll off your shoulders, stop reading reviews, or ..."

Just as I was about to make an excuse, my other line clicked in.

"Sorry, Kay—hold that thought. My other line is ringing."

With the way my morning had started off, the last thing I wanted to do was answer my phone. I had every intention of letting it go to voicemail, but the same number had buzzed in over five times. While it was agitating me even more, as I wasn't done whining my point at Kay, I thought I'd better see what the emergency was.

"This is Kristy, can I help you?" I answered with a tad of attitude.

"Is this Kristy, the one on the radio?" A young voice asked.

"Yes, how can I help you?" I repeated, wondering if perhaps one of the naysayers was going to start calling me. That was all I needed.

"Umm...I heard you on the radio and thought maybe you could help me," the girl said, and broke down into sobs.

I forgot all about Kay on the other line and immediately went into intuitive mode.

"Want to talk about it?" I asked, gently.

For the next half hour, the fifteen-year-old, who told me that her name was Taryn, confessed to me her troubles. Everything from struggling in school because of a learning disability to feeling liking an outcast and not having any friends, to seeing her mom struggle with money.

She told me that she had pretended to be sick to stay home from school, with intentions of killing herself. "Maybe if I was just gone then my mom wouldn't struggle as much," she reasoned.

My heart skipped a few beats and I started to tear up.

"I am a mom, Taryn, and I know for a fact that you being gone wouldn't help at all. She works a lot?"

Taryn told me her mom's first name and the place where she worked, so I quietly grabbed my husband from his home office, gave him a note with the circumstances on it, the young girl's mom's name and employment name, and asked him to Google it and to call her immediately as I stayed on the phone. Chuck nodded to me that he got hold of her and mouthed that she was on her way home.

So I stayed on the phone. Taryn and I talked about how she felt alone and how she didn't have any friends. She said that she had turned on the radio as she was contemplating how to end her life when my segment came on. When she couldn't get through, she said she felt abandoned again, but she took a chance on contacting me afterward.

I certainly was glad that she did.

"What's the Other Side like, Kristy?"

I hesitated. If I told her the truth, that it was beautiful and without pain, I feared she would take her life. Although it was the truth, many that came to see me in spirit after committing suicide explained that it was a lot of work at first. It wasn't an instant Heaven, but a soul journey that they had to explore, and a Hell, in a way, as they had to witness the pain that their loved ones had to deal with at their own hand. I was stuck with what the right words were to say. I was stalling. But then a presence came to me.

"Taryn, did your dad kill himself? I have a man in spirit that is standing next to me. He has on a work shirt, sort of like what you would see a mechanic wearing, and dirty jeans."

I heard Taryn suck in her breath and begin to cry. "That would be my daddy. I just want to be with him."

"Oh Taryn," I said, my heart aching. I looked over at the man for help. He was handsome. Dark brown hair, slicked back, with cocoa-colored eyes.

"Tell her that I regret what I did every single day. I was stupid. I was depressed and I wasn't thinking of anybody else. I was a selfish person and I ended my life selfishly. She is smarter than I am. She is more loving than I am and she has so much more to pursue than I ever did."

I didn't quite agree with everything he said. I felt as if this man was still making excuses for his life and for his death, but I gave Taryn the message verbatim.

"I want you to tell her five things. Ready?"

I nodded and began writing, asking if Taryn was still with me. She sobbed that she was. And I began to write and give the information to Taryn as I multi-tasked.

1. There's always hope, even if you feel hopeless. You will and you can get through this.

2. Give yourself twenty-four hours before you ever do anything drastic in your life. Emotions and actions are two separate things and they often cannot be combined at the same time.

3. You are in pain right now. But pain is a feeling and sometimes a good feeling because it helps to differentiate what is what.

4. Many people will react badly to your suicidal feelings for of an array of reasons. They might be scared

and they might even be angry, mainly because they will think that they have done you wrong. But your feelings are your feelings. There are people who will be with you through this time, though. They will not judge you, but will only try to do the best for you.

5. Never ever think that you are alone or unloved.

"I did what I had to do, Taryn," her dad said. "And yes, I do have regrets for hurting you and your mom, but I will forever be with you. I'm not ready for you over here. I can't wait to see what you accomplish over there."

"But is he okay?" Taryn asked me.

"He's okay. If he could come through to give you this lecture—he's just fine. Do you ever feel him around you?" I asked her.

"I think so. I sometimes feel my hair being touched and it never freaked me out. I can remember being little and my dad brushing my hair, so I thought maybe it was him."

I looked over at Taryn's dad and he simply smiled and nodded his head yes.

"Did you feel him there with you this morning when you called me?"

I didn't hear a response and I got scared for a second. "Taryn?"

"Sorry, my mom just walked in. Yeah, I felt my hair being touched when I was listening to the radio this morning. So he's really with me?"

"Absolutely! Trust," I smiled into the phone. "Can I talk to your mom?" I asked her, worried that she would just hang up, but Taryn handed the phone to her mom and we spoke briefly. I asked her to keep me updated and she did. Taryn got help with her grief and depression and every so often sends me updates.

Taryn is now in college and studying psychology, hoping to help others that felt as alone as she did. And she still feels her dad brushing her hair; even though there is no scientific reasoning to the how or the who—she knows.

My guides sure schooled me that day for my griping over something so petty, and put life in perspective for me in a big way. I am so grateful that I was in the right place at the right time, and I thank the radio station for having faith in me and having me on in the first place. My life wasn't bad. My kids were healthy and happy. Sure, we've had our ups and downs (haven't we all?), but the negativity of one little situation enveloped me for an hour of my life. An hour too long.

So when you are upset over something, or you are feeling like the world has gotten you down, know that the situation is there to learn from. Oftentimes the situation has greater expectations and bigger motives than originally thought. And as you can see, I am not perfect (darn it!) and I sometimes allow myself to only see the clouds in front, forgetting that the rainbows are all around. It can take time, or action to see through the denseness of the yuck, and I know that it takes work.

My mom used to say, "Someone else always has it worse than us." So, ask yourself when you are in that situation, if life is *really* that bad, or if you are putting on the tiara and being a Drama Queen (or King). And when all else fails, I can lease out Kay to you, I am sure she wouldn't mind.

Suicide Is Not the Answer

Suicide is not the answer. It is never the answer. But we have to be realistic: it happens. When I receive inquiries from those contemplating suicide and inquiries whether or not they will go to a good place if they go through with it, I tell them the truth. I am never sure, and because of that uncertainty, why would they take the gamble? Instead it is best to look for help and healing here.

If you are having suicidal thoughts, you're not alone; many have had suicidal thoughts at some point in their life. Feeling suicidal is not a character defect, and it doesn't mean that you are crazy or weak. It only means that you have more pain than you can cope with at that point in time. The pain may seem permanent, but with time and support, the pain and the suicidal thoughts can be healed.

If you don't know who to turn to:

+ In the U.S.—Call the National Suicide Prevention Lifeline at 1-800-273-TALK (8255) or the
  National Hopeline Network at 1-800-SUICIDE
  (1-800-784-2433). These toll-free crisis hotlines
  offer 24-hour suicide prevention and support.
  Your call is free and confidential.

+ You can also chat with someone at the Suicidal Prevention Lifeline at suicidepreventionlifeline.org

+ Outside the U.S.—Visit International Association for Suicide Prevention (www.iasp.info) or suicide.org to find a helpline in your country.

Chapter Twelve

A Spirit's Touch

The feeling of your hair being stroked, tingles down your spine, a soft touch down your arms, or slight pressure on your leg can be an indication that a loved one on the Other Side is near you.

Nelly

"Mom, you really need new furniture! Dale received a bonus check last week, let us buy you a new couch, and maybe a new chair too," Sarah said, as she sat down in her mom's living room.

Nelly looked around her well-loved but worn home. She was proud of her house. She raised three boys and one daughter in a three-bedroom, one-bath ranch, and spent over fifty very happy years with their dad, her sweetheart, there. But when Ray passed away five years ago, she just didn't care so much about what things looked like, including herself and most of all her furniture.

The plaid couch, although out of style, was where she used to give Ray his nighttime coffee. When he got sick, he would sit there and she would cover him with his favorite blanket, give him his pills, and they would talk about their younger days, and laugh and smile. That brown couch was where Ray took his last breath. Sarah didn't know it, but every night, Nelly would curl up on that eyesore of an itchy sofa and pretend that she could still hear Ray breathing, smell his soap, and sometimes, well, sometimes she thought she could feel him touch her arm.

"I don't need anything new, honey. I don't get company except for you and the kids, and I am comfortable."

Sarah sighed. She'd seen her mom fade after her dad passed away, and although Nelly's house wasn't dirty, it was messy, which was highly unusual for her mom's personality. Sarah knew it was depression, grief, and sadness, but she wanted to help. She followed her mom into the kitchen to help fix some hot tea.

"And look at this refrigerator, Mom! This Christmas card is three years old!" Sarah took a photo off with Merry Christmas 2000 on it and tossed it in the trash.

"Oh, is it?" Nelly said, absently, while putting two cinnamon tea bags into the teacups.

"Leaving things like this won't bring dad back, ya know? What it's doing is taking up room for new things to happen. You, yourself, used to say that we needed to leave room in our hearts for God to fill it with the good. Do you think you deserve bad?"

Nelly choked back the tears and quickly changed the subject to Sarah's work. Sarah knew her mom well enough to know when to drop a sore subject.

When dusk fell that evening, Nelly crawled onto the couch with Ray's blanket wrapped tightly around her. "I don't know if I deserve anything good to fill my heart," she cried. "How could I possibly deserve more good than what I had?" Oh, sure, not everything had been wonderful, but Nelly always tried to turn it into a positive, that is what Ray loved so much about her. The moment she buried her husband, she buried her will to see things in a positive light. She filled her heart space up with sadness and grief. As she pondered it all, she felt Ray softly touch her arm and she heard him say, *make space, Nell, make space.*

She cried herself to sleep on the couch that night, wishing and hoping that the last five years had just been an awful nightmare.

The next morning she woke up stiff, but feeling a bit lighter, a bit freer. As she made her morning tea, she looked at the cluttered refrigerator, and little by little began to organize the menus, photos, and past-due bills into a pile to either file or pitch. She took a dishrag and wiped down the refrigerator door, horrified at the dust and dirt, and with fresh eyes looked around at her space to see—there just was none; the space was all taken up. She spent the rest of the day throwing out old newspapers, food, junk mail, and the like. And as she sat down on the couch, she called Sarah.

"I heard what you said yesterday, Sarah, and I understand. I would like to take you up on your offer."

Before Sarah's mom could change her mind, Sarah raced over to the house and took Nelly to the furniture store, where they picked out a tasteful (and comfortable) tan couch and recliner chair.

As they placed it in the living room, pushing the old furniture aside, Sarah looked at her mom. "You okay?"

Nelly nodded, and with tears in her eyes, took scissors and carefully began to cut away the material on the old couch.

Sarah looked on confused.

"I am going to wash this and then make pillows. Not all old needs to be tossed—there is room for both."

Sarah smiled and took another pair of scissors and began to assist.

"Have you ever felt Dad around?" Sarah hesitantly asked her mom. They were raised in a religion that taught once you die, you go to Heaven until you meet again.

Nelly stopped cutting and set the scissors on the coffee table that Ray had built years back when they had no money and he had ambition. "I do, Sarah. I feel Dad around, especially when I go to bed. I have felt him touch me and I know it is him."

Sarah had felt her dad, too, but was always afraid to talk about it.

A Kiss

I was asked to give a presentation at a local high school on psychics and the paranormal. Teenagers are extremely inquisitive and intelligent and I get a great deal of satisfaction from sharing my stories with them.

As I was talking, I caught sight of a man in spirit sitting next to what I believed to be his daughter or granddaughter. He was dressed in a snazzy-looking tweed suit and a matching hat. His face was dusted with salt-and-pepper-colored whiskers and every so often, I would see him lean over to the young girl and whisper in her ear and affectionately give her a peck on the cheek. In return, she would swat at the air and brush the tickle off her face. I was having a hard time not saying anything, but I wasn't there to give readings, and I didn't feel it was proper without the parents' permission. After the hour, several of the kids came up to me to ask me different questions, and some offered me a hug and a thank you. As I gathered my bag, I noticed the same girl hovering in the hallway, outside of the classroom. I smiled at her as I started walking down the hall toward the doorway.

"Ms. Robinett, can I walk with you?" she asked me, and I smiled and obliged. "Can I ask you something?"

I nodded in agreement, already knowing what she was going to ask.

"My dad was killed when I was just three years old. Is he ever around me?" Her eyes filled with tears, as did mine.

I stopped at the exit and turned to look at her beautiful brown eyes and looked over at her dad, who bent down to kiss her like I had seen him do in the classroom. And once again, she touched her face to itch it.

"Right there, that feeling on your face, Kayla, that is your dad giving you a kiss. He's always with you."

The young girl's eyes grew large with both fear and surprise. "Where is he? Can you position me to him?"

So I posed her in front of her dad where she went on her tiptoes, put her arms around his shoulders and gave the spirit of her dad a kiss. "Did I get him?"

"Yep, you sure did."

Without another word, Kayla turned around and skipped into her next class.

Conclusion

I Believe

I believe that we all have the gift of sight with the ability to have after-death communication with our loved ones. I am not special. I do not have a super power. The sixth sense is something real. It doesn't mean that you have to hang up a flashy psychic sign on your office door. Intuition, sensing, knowing, and gut feelings, whatever you want to call it, are within each one of us. You may not physically see your loved ones, but they are there and try to show themselves in so many different ways.

None of us have the complete road map in front of us in this world, or in the next, but we have an inner GPS that helps guide us. It is that turn-by-turn direction that we all have, but we doubt and create false scenarios in our head, especially if there is a lot of gray around us. It makes it easier to point fingers at others than to own the burden of responsibility. And yet when we get burned, we punish ourselves because we knew. When a knowing can't be explained, we instead attempt to rationalize it.

And so people go to see mediums, psychics, and life coaches to validate the knowing. Most of the time my clients don't need me, or any psychic or medium. Yes, I said it. They don't. They merely need to trust that their inner GPS is synced and giving them correct directions, yet hearing it from another source helps to inspire and lessens some of the responsibility through the decisions. We each have free will. We each have free choice. The choice is up to you to embrace your knowing, but it is also your choice to follow through on your knowing.

In a session with a client, her loved one on the Other Side showed me a large tree with dead branches. "They need to be trimmed," her mom told me to communicate. "The foundation is still good. The roots are still there, but they won't be for long if the dead isn't cut off."

Her mom wasn't talking about gardening, but instead all of the junk in life that we keep around just because. Those grudges. Hurtful e-mails and text messages. The names and phone numbers in our phone book of past friends and scorned lovers who won't ever serve us any good in the future. Hurtful memories that have kept us from moving forward, or from reuniting with loved ones, or from finding another job. Sadness, disappointment, ego, and/or jealousies. However you label it, it continues to kill the very thing that helps us flourish. We continue to allow the many branches that come off of our soul to stay there even when they are hollowed and taking precious nourishment, when all we have to do is cut off the dead wood. You will always remember how beautiful those branches were when they were whole but by cutting them you gain a stronger foundation to grow those limbs into healthier paths. And then, and only then, after time new blooms can appear. But by protecting what isn't worthy of being protected—oftentimes we are afraid to make the changes—we are slowly killing our soul and our spirit because of that fear.

Having prolonged negativity eats away at you, from the inside out. Each one of us deserves a happy life and Afterlife.

How to Get Rid of the Dead Wood:

1. Prune—Clean out your e-mail box,
   your text messages, your phone book, etc.

2. Plant—Shift your focus to the
   blooms that you want to have.

3. Fertilize—Release what you don't want in your life by
   writing out a grudge list. Then say out loud, "I release
   _____." Keep or burn the list, giving it over to the
   Universe. And then reaffirm what you do want.

4. Harvest—It may take time, but blossoms
   and then fruit will appear on your new
   limbs. Express gratitude and thanks.

When the dead branches are cut, the true connections are created. Never give up on reaching out to your loved ones on the Other Side. Their signs to you come in countless different ways. Many are very subtle and can easily be missed, or we may think it's wishful thinking when it's really a sign. Keep asking your loved ones for a specific sign, but be open to any type of signs. They want to share with you what a wonderful Afterlife it is, not to brag or make you feel bad, but to reassure you that they are okay.

Remember that our love for them never dies, nor does theirs for us, even from the Afterlife.

Appendix

Grounding

Many of us miss the signs and symbols because we are bombarded with all the worldly *noise* around us. Symptoms of being ungrounded* include:

+ anxiety with no cause

+ cannot focus

+ sudden dizziness

+ falling asleep while meditating

+ inability to sleep

+ heaviness in the body

+ feeling spacey

+ feeing emotional

- craving sugar
- wanting to just eat junk food
- nausea
- mental confusion
- inability to focus on simple tasks

*Note: See your doctor and use common sense, as some of these symptoms can be caused by a medical condition.

Time Out Suggestions

1. Rid yourself of negative people.
2. Unplug every so often.
3. Embrace nature—take a walk, a bike ride, garden, etc.
4. Trust your intuition.
5. Read a book.
6. Put on some music.
7. Meditate.
8. Create. Something. Anything!
9. Clean up loose ends.
10. Spend time with positive people.

Five Ways to Ground Yourself

1. Get in water—sit in a hot tub or warm bath.

2. Get into nature—hug a tree, take your shoes off and walk, or garden.

3. Meditate or do pilates or yoga.

4. Utilize crystals—smoky quartz, Black Tourmaline, hematite, to name a few.

5. Eat raw foods.

So whether you are feeling ungrounded, or feel as if you are being haunted, remember that not everyone who wanders is lost—including your loved ones on the Other Side. They are just stopping in to say hello.

Re-Aligning Your Spirit to Connect With Their Spirit

Our loved ones in spirit are around us if we so choose to invite them. They want to help us as much as they can and are capable of (which is actually more than you might think). And if you don't have a loved one on the Other Side, we all have Spirit Guides who act as our best friend from the Other Side, assisting in life's challenges and celebrations. Building that relationship is key. Just as relationships change with past coworkers when you move on to another job or family/friends when they move to another state, the same is true for those on the Other Side. You have to be proactive in building the relationship. It gets tiring always being the one trying to initiate (our poor Spirit Guides and Guardians!) and secure that relationship. So, spend some time talking to, inviting, and loving. And although our loved ones have jobs on the Other Side, they are just a whisper away when you need them.

Sometimes the connection is lacking because you are unaligned with your own spirit. Some may call it bad luck, but it is actually negative energy that can cause life to turn upside down, or at least feel that way. Depression, fear, anger, arguments, psychic vampires (negative people), sadness, unhappiness, etc., clings like saran wrap to your aura field and attracts more of the same situations, along with exhaustion, fatigue, unhappiness, an unsettled feeling, and sometimes even health conditions. Just as a furnace filter needs to be replaced or cleansed, so does your energy filter. How often you need to complete an energy cleanse is dependent upon your personal and professional situation.

There are numerous ways that you can cleanse yourself, your office, your home, and even your car. Anywhere that you spend your time is fair game to have residual energy—good and bad—attach to you.

Ways to Cleanse Yourself

Brush Off

Brush yourself with hands diagonally across the body from fingertips, down arms, down legs, and torso, and then throw all "bad" energy on the floor to get rid of it. You can visualize a drain by your feet where it departs.

Crystals

Crystals are said to have healing properties. They can raise your vibration and cleanse stress and tension from your spirit.

White Light Protection

Visualize an egg-shaped sphere of brilliant white light that completely surrounds you from head to toe. Visualize the light getting brighter and brighter until it creates a barrier of protection around you. Depending upon your religious beliefs, you can simply say a prayer or ask for your guides and angels to continue to surround you with the white light of protection, and that it keeps you from harm and negative influences. You can also do this for others, including pets.

Bathe

Sea salt is used to neutralize the environment and oneself. If possible, get unrefined sea salt, along with Epsom salts (and you can even mix with your herbs). Draw a warm bath and relax. When you are done, drain the bath but don't hop out; instead, think of all the things that are troubling you, and visualize them drawing from your body and draining with the water, until every drop of it is gone.

Ways to Cleanse the Home

Reiki

Draw Reiki symbols with hands/fingers to clear spaces. It is important to draw the symbols on walls, ceilings, windows, doorways, and floors. Just follow your intuition to guide you to what should be cleansed.

Herbs

Many herbs, such as basil, lavender, peppermint, rosemary, sage, and cinnamon have protective qualities against negativity. You can set them out in a pretty dish to help absorb the negativity, you can burn the herbs by using incenses of those properties, and you can bathe with them.

Smudging

Smudging with sage (I prefer white sage) is a simple and powerful way in which to remove negative energy from the area. Place a few leaves in a fireproof container or an albacore shell, and light the leaves or light the bundle. The flame should go out in a short time, and the sage will begin to smolder. Fan the smoke with your hand or a feather. Say a blessing of protection, or prayer, as you walk around. Fan the smoke around you, imagining it passing through you. It flows through you, drawing out all of the imperfections that have collected within you. I recommend going to the farthest part of your house and working toward the front, opening a window where you can draw all of the negative energy out. Don't forget to smudge closets, basements, nooks, and crevices, etc.

Smudging yourself on a daily basis can also be very helpful in keeping yourself balanced, and can help if you are around emotionally unbalanced people.

Frankincense, sandalwood, myrrh, and Palo Santo also work to remove negativity.

Holy Water

Those of certain faith practices believe that making the sign of the cross with holy water in and around the house helps to call on the Divine in order to dispel negative energy.

Sea Salt

Place a glass or bowl of water with sea salt in it in a corner or under the bed to capture negative energies. Dump and replace each day. Dumping to Mother Earth helps to transmute the negative to positive.

Candles

White candles work wonderfully to remove negative energy, and adding scents to the candles, such as lavender, vanilla, and cinnamon, helps even more.

Music

Since we all have a vibration, it makes sense that music can help realign our soul. Playing an instrument yourself, or simply putting on your favorite music, and spending time thinking of all that you want instead of what you don't want, can help re-tune your space and your spirit.

Ways to Cleanse the Office

Most offices don't love an open flame, so visualization works best when you work in a populated place.

Visualize a vortex swirling around, and ask that all negative and/or dark energies be picked up by the vortex. Then visualize the vortex moving throughout the office building until it exits out your roof. Ask that the angels and guides neutralize and dissipate them. Don't forget to thank them.

No matter how you decide to cleanse yourself, your home, or your office, know that positive attracts positive, and when you are around any type of negative situation or person, in some form, it will begin to weigh on you. Although you cannot see the energy, others can sense it. Spending just a small amount of time doing self-care and soul cleansing could end up changing your life, along with opening up the channels of communication with your loved ones.

Common Questions

Question: I heard that when people cross over, everyone is aged at around thirty-two. Is that true or are they at the age they passed?

Answer: When we cross over, we don't have any age. Our soul and spirit are timeless. We often emit the age that we were the happiest at in this earthly plane.

Question: What if a baby dies? Who takes care of them in the Afterlife?

Answer: A baby or child is greeted just the same as an adult, by a guide, angel, and/or a loved one, even if they hadn't met that person or people in their earthly existence. They are taken care of until they reunite with their parents in Heaven and they, too, are offered the choice of reincarnation.

Question: Do we have "bodies" like we do
   here? Like do we have arms and legs or
   are we just energy blobs floating around?

Answer: No, we don't have bodies.
   We are merely made up of energy.

Question: Are all dogs really in Heaven?

Answer: Animals do go to Heaven! Not all of them,
   though. Have you ever met a dog or a cat (or
   horse or snake, etc.) and knew that there was
   something special about them, and then met a dog
   or a cat and felt that they were just a dog or a cat?

Question: I experienced my dad crossing over in a dream;
   it was several years after his death. But I saw my
   mom cross just after a few days. Why the difference?

Answer: Your dad might have felt bad about
   his passing, or he was afraid to cross.

Question: Who gets to go to the "Other Side" or
   Heaven, and who gets to go to "Limbo" or Hell?
   How is that decided? Are murderers and child
   abusers just hanging out on the other side
   enjoying time with their loved ones?

Answer: Heaven (and Hell) is created much like an
   apartment building, with many different realms
   and floors. You only have an elevator key
   for your own floor, and no others.

Question: When we are about to die, are our loved ones in Heaven aware and waiting to greet us? Do they hear? Do they know already? Do they help us?

Answer: It is almost as if our loved ones get the memo a few days before our passing, even if it is from an accident or something unexpected, so that they can be there for the reunion.

Question: Do you wear what you were buried in?

Answer: We don't really wear anything—we aren't physical. For me, I see them in the clothes they are most comfortable in or that can be most validated.

Question: How soon can our loved ones "find their voice" and start communicating to their loved ones on this side?

Answer: It typically takes six months to a year for our loved ones to find their voice, but that depends upon how ready they were to die and cross over.

Question: Is the transition from life to Heaven a frightening experience?

Answer: Not at all.

Question: What happens if you're cremated?

Answer: The same as if you were buried. We are made up of energy and how we are put to rest has no impact on our soul or spirit.

Question: Do we reincarnate, or just stay in Heaven?

Answer: We reincarnate only if we want to.

Question: In the Bible we hear that there are many mansions in Heaven. Do people describe them?

Answer: Everyone on the Other Side has a different experience of what they see. Their Heaven is what they want it to be. If someone is religious, they will see the Biblical views of what they were taught.

Question: The things we enjoy in this life, the places we love to visit … are we still able to enjoy those things and do those things? Or, are those types of earthly activities no longer desired?

Answer: We are absolutely able to enjoy life and the places that we enjoyed on this earthly plane. We often enjoy that through our loved ones on Earth. So, if you vacation in Hawaii and your dad always loved Hawaii, it is almost a sure thing that he is hitchhiking along.

Question: Can our loved ones in Heaven help us?

Answer: Absolutely. They can move mountains for us, but you have to ask them to. They aren't all-knowing and they have rules and regulations on the Other Side too. So, invite them in, ask for their assistance, and then wait for their response. It may not be the timing you would like, but it will come.

Question: Do we get to be with our loved ones
   in Heaven?

Answer: Most of the time, yes. It depends upon the Soul
   Review and the choices during Angel Boot Camp.

Question: Do our loved ones keep up with what's
   happening to us in our lives as time goes on here?
   Like do they know when we marry, have a child,
   or when something bad happens in our lives?

Answer: Yes, they do know what's happening in our life.

"I Am Always With You"
Anonymous

When I am gone, release me, let me go.
I have so many things to see and do,
You mustn't tie yourself to me with too many tears,
But be thankful we had so many good years.

I gave you my love, and you can only guess
How much you've given me in happiness.
I thank you for the love that you have shown,
But now it is time I traveled on alone.

So grieve for me a while, if grieve you must
Then let your grief be comforted by trust
That it is only for a while that we must part,
So treasure the memories within your heart.

I won't be far away for life goes on.
And if you need me, call and I will come.
Though you can't see or touch me, I will be near
And if you listen with your heart, you'll hear
All my love around you soft and clear

And then, when you come this way alone,
I'll greet you with a smile and a "Welcome Home."

Making the Connection With the Other Side

1. Find a place where you can be alone and in the quiet for ten to fifteen minutes. Some of my favorite places to escape are my car, a cemetery, the bathtub, etc. It often helps create a ritual of sorts—the same time, the same place, etc.

2. You might want to bring out pictures or mementos of the loved one you want to talk to.

3. You might want to light a white candle and/or put on calming music.

4. Call on God, your higher self, and/or spirit guides.

5. Use a form of spiritual protection.*

6. Repeat the affirmation: *Nothing can enter my space without my permission.*

7. And simply breathe in and out, tuning the world out and tuning in.

8. Invite your loved one in. Call out to them in your head or out loud, whatever feels most comfortable.

9. You might want to have a notebook by your side and jot down or write down any thoughts or information that comes to mind. Or just simply listen, feel, and take in all of the senses.

10. Just as you know a loved one's personality and idiosyncrasies, our personalities do not change when we cross over, and you should be able to sense and get a feel for whether who comes through is your loved one. If you feel uncomfortable or unsure, stop the communication, and begin again with the spiritual protection.

At first, don't spend more than fifteen minutes, as it can be emotionally and psychically draining to both you and your loved one.

*Psychic or spiritual protection acts as a form of energy that wraps around us in order to block lower-level or malicious energies. Just because you might want to talk to your grandma and only your grandma in the spirit world, it doesn't mean that another nosy spirit being doesn't want to, or can't butt in on the conversation. It's not about being harmed by an entity, but it is a means of dialing the phone and not having a party line with multiple people, which can confuse and frustrate the messages from the person that you are attempting to connect with.

Protection Techniques

White Bubble Technique

The most basic technique for protection is to simply imagine yourself inside a ball or bubble of white light. Visualize this bubble of white light coming down from the ceiling, all the way on top of your head, and wrapping you with this white light all the way down to your feet, at least six inches below your feet. It doesn't have to be a perfect sphere; just make it fit around your entire body in whatever shape seems most comfortable to you. You can also join others into your bubble, or connect your bubble to others. Visualize the light getting brighter and brighter until it creates a barrier of protection around you. Depending upon your religious beliefs, you can simply say a prayer or ask for your guides and angels to continue to surround you with the white light of protection, and that it keeps you from harm and negative influences. You can also do this for others, including pets.

Mummy Technique

Just as some people like lightweight blankets on them, others like a heavy blanket. The mummy protection is much like the white bubble, but instead of being within a bubble, take the energy of that bubble and wrap yourself in it. Visualize a white light ribbon and wrap yourself tightly from head to toe. Depending upon your religious beliefs, you can simply say a prayer or ask for your guides and angels to continue to surround you with the white light of protection and that it keeps you from harm and negative influences.

Rain Technique

Visualize a light rain coming from the heavens, over the top of you. As the spiritual rain hits your head, it gently drips down around your body, surrounding you with protection. Depending upon your religious beliefs, you can simply say a prayer or ask for your guides and angels to continue to surround you with the spiritual rain of protection and that it keeps you from harm and negative influences.

Live on Purpose: Seven Regrets of the Dead and Dying

1. I wish I had done more things that made me happy. And they rarely mean anything from a monetary sense. You've heard of a bucket list? It is a list of goals that you want to accomplish, but different from a "to do" list. Bucket lists are personal and unique to each person. I had a client who was battling cancer and knew that her time was limited. In our session she shared her bucket list with me and I still to this day think of it.

    › Buy a stranger lunch.

    › Put random notes in library books.

    › Watch a sunset and sunrise on the same day.

    › Swim with dolphins.

    › Hold a koala bear.

> Stay at a B&B on Lake Michigan.

> Learn how to play an instrument.

> Take a painting class.

> Go to an old-fashioned county
fair and eat elephant ears.

> Visit a medium.

> Ride in a hot air balloon.

> Take the autumn train ride to the Upper Peninsula.

The items on her list weren't earth-shattering, but they were hers. She sent me pictures along the way on her bucket list journey and I loved sharing it with her.

2. I wish I had traveled/explored more.
Many times fear stops us from traveling and exploring, even moreso than money. What's the saying—if wishes were fishes? Well, there is also the saying that says to live your life on purpose. Don't allow for chance, instead create and complete.

3. I wish I had kept in touch with my friends.
My mom often spoke of her friends and relatives and expressed how much she missed them. I would tell her to call them, but she would respond, "The telephone lines work both ways." She grew bitter and felt forgotten. But near the end of her life, she would talk about how she wished she would have picked up the

phone, or written a note (or had me write the note as she was blind). It isn't too late to send that text, or send a card, write a note, or make that call. Even if you haven't talked to your friend in forever, no matter the circumstances, if they are still on your mind maybe it is time to reconnect.

4. I wish I hadn't spent so much time working.

One of my favorite lines is from W. James "Jim" Treliving, a Canadian businessman, owner of Boston Pizza and author of *Decisions: Making the Right Ones, Righting the Wrong Ones*. He is quoted as saying that you never see a Brinks truck following a hearse. Yes, bills need to be paid, but look at the depth of those bills. Are you having to work hard for sensible shoes or working overtime to buy a Louis Vuitton bag? What is quality to you?

5. I should've taken better care of myself.

I hear so many on the Other Side say that they wish they would've gone to the doctor at the first sign of a problem. Or that they should have eaten better, or exercised—yes, they do even say they wish they would have exercised. It isn't that they aren't okay now, but they feel remorseful for leaving their family and friends.

6. I should've told the people that I loved how much I truly loved them.

I should've, would've, could've … Love is probably
the hardest word to say for many. The next one is—
"I'm so proud of you." But the sentiment can
change someone's life, and the person speaking it.

7. I wish I wouldn't have spent so much time worrying.
Worry kills happiness. It steals time. It pushes people
away. And it causes health issues. Worrying also doesn't
affect the outcome of what you are worrying about.

Don't you (and I) have the responsibility to live the
happiest, the fullest, and the most authentic life ever?
As much as we want to blame our unhappiness on
work, or others, or lack of money, or whatever else we
can point the finger at—it all comes down to creating
our life. You have the paint brush and a blank canvas.
It's up to when, or if, you begin to color your life.

Visitation Meditation Before Bed

(It may help for you to take this script and record it on your
phone and play it for yourself.)

Grounding is important to release all of the stress and to
break down the barriers between this side and the Other Side.

Begin breathing slowly and deeply, with in-breath and
out-breath of approximately the same length. Shrug or roll
your shoulders, carefully roll your head around your neck,
and try to tense and relax all the major muscles of your
body, starting with your feet and working to your face.

Imagine roots coming out of your legs and the bottom of your feet and going into a cool and moist soil. With each out-breath, your roots grow and reach deeper into the soil. Feel all of your stress and tension flow out of your roots with each out-breath. Continue to focus on extending your roots into Mother Earth. And as you release your stress, Mother Earth energizes you through every cell in your body from your feet all the way up to your head and through the crown of your head.

Stretch your arms up toward the ceiling, toward the sky, toward the sun; with each out breath, your branches reach further into the sky, continuing to release all of your tension and stress.

Now visualize a doorway in front of you. When you open this doorway, see yourself on a path. This path may take on any form you wish. Notice the sound of nature that lives within it; the birds and the bees, and any other animals that may be scurrying about. Visualize yourself walking down the peaceful path. You might feel the wind against your cheek, or feel the warm sun shining down on you. As you walk, you come to a bridge and on the other side of this bridge are your loved ones who have crossed over. Invite them to meet you in the middle of the bridge, and then slowly walk onto the bridge and allow yourself to be greeted by who comes. You may just sense, not see, but the more you do this meditation, the clearer it will be.

Don't second-guess yourself or think that you are wishing for that certain person to be there, just let it happen. Spend only a few minutes on the bridge; offer your love and any messages that you want to share. Listen for a moment to see if they share one in return, and then turn around and go back down the path and through your doorway. Remember that the more you do this, the easier this meditation and the communication becomes. Don't allow frustration to hinder anything that you see or feel.

Take a deep breath and open your eyes, or simply allow yourself to go to sleep.

Holiday Healings: Five Ways to Celebrate the Holidays While Missing

The holidays can make the missing even more painful. Instead of feeling jolly, a pasted-on smile and a sense of dread and sadness is the norm. Those that have never encountered this type of a heartache just won't get it, but for those who have—it can be debilitating.

Whether the loss happened ten years ago, or two weeks ago, it hurts, and the void of that presence during the holidays can be painful beyond words. Friends and family may think they are helping with suggestions like, "Oh, just come on out, you will feel better!" and "It was so long ago, can't you just move on?" and "Well, they are in a better place!" but it just doesn't heal the situation. And no, they can't bring them back or make it all better, but you can. We choose our attitude. We choose our mood. We choose to take steps forward, even if tiny ones.

I can still remember my mom crying every holiday, but especially at Christmas. She had lost both of her brothers, her mom, and then her dad. She felt orphaned. And although she had my dad, me, and my brother and sister, we could never take away her sadness, nor did she have any energy to work on healing it. When her family was alive, our Christmas Eves were filled with laughter, family, good food, and happiness—but the losses turned what had been such a fun and joyful day into one that felt contrived and forced. Mom's tears fell easily and her heart never did emotionally heal. After all these years, I can still feel torn about Christmas. As a child I sorely wanted to feel the holiday magic, but I knew that the magic was dulled with losses and much sadness. I tried to be the cheerleader, but it got tiring. And then when I experienced my own losses, my spark dulled until I took the time to restore it and I couldn't be there for everyone else.

Despite my own ability to communicate with my own loved ones, I know firsthand that it isn't the same as a big hug in the physical world.

Set a Positive Trigger

When you start feeling sad, have a happy go-to. It could be putting on a movie that always makes you laugh, playing a song that makes you smile, visiting a place that makes you feel good, etc.

Pay It Forward

When we help others, and see them smile back, it makes us feel good too. There are numerous ways to do this:

+ Pay for the order of the car behind you.

+ Put change in an empty parking meter.

+ Bake cookies and gift them to a neighbor, your doctor's office, coworkers, the church, etc.

+ Clean out your closet and donate items to a worthy cause.

+ Write a book review and post it on Amazon (believe me—the author will be very grateful).

+ Volunteer at an animal shelter or nursing home.

+ Smile at a stranger.

+ Shovel a neighbor's walk.

Create a New Tradition

Death leaves a void within the traditions that brings out the pain. So often we think that the pain we encounter by keeping the tradition is worth it, but in the end it's we who suffer. Create a new tradition—whether it is the food, the decorations, or even the location where the festivities are held. Freshen up the festivities.

Don't Ignore the Pain

This may sound counterproductive from what I previously said, but by ignoring it, you are only allowing it to one day surface, and when it does, the mountain will be even larger.

Sit down and write your passed loved one a letter or simply talk to them. They hear you. Believe me.

Talk about the person you are missing. Find the happy memories—the ones that made you laugh.

Include Those Who've Passed

During the time I was sad, Chuck (my husband) and I decided to take a drive. We stopped at a small Christmas store and there in the window was a lantern like the ones my mom used to collect. I knew I had to have it. As the lady lovingly wrapped it up for me I told her it reminded me of the collection my mom had and I went on to say that my mom had passed away, and that Christmas time was always the hardest. I reached into my wallet to hand her my credit card when she simply shook her head, smiled, and handed me the bag—"A gift from me and your mom," she said to me as tears formed in my eyes. Not only did I feel close to my mom at that moment, but my faith was once again restored in people.

The lantern sits right next to me as I write to remind me of many things that are far more than objects. Visit the places that remind you of your loved one, maybe even buy a gift for them during the holidays, or set a place at the table for them. They miss you just as much as you miss them.

Missing during the holidays is natural and it is important to communicate your emotions instead of avoiding them. It is then that healing comes.

"I'm Always Here"
Anonymous

I have not turned my back on you,
So there is no need to cry.
I'm watching you from Heaven,
Just beyond the morning sky.

I've seen you almost fall apart,
When you could barely stand.
I asked the Lord to comfort you,
And watched him take your hand.

He told me you are in more pain,
Than I could ever be.
He wiped his eyes and swallowed hard,
Then gave your hand to me.

Although you may not feel my touch,
Or see me by your side.
I've whispered that I love you,
While I wiped each tear you cried.

So please try not to ache for me,
We'll meet again one day.
Beyond the dark and stormy sky,
A rainbow lights the way.

References

Australian Museum. "Death: The Last Taboo," Victorian Era. http://www.deathonline.net/remembering/mourning/victorian.cfm

Breedlove, Ally. Ben Breedlove funeral—sister Ally's speech, December 31, 2011.

Farmer, Steven D. *Animal Spirit Guides: An Easy-to-Use Handbook for Identifying and Understanding Your Spirit Animals and Animal Spirit Helpers.* Hay House, 2006.

Jacon, Alain. *What Is Hell Like? Biblical Record Confirmed by Personal Narratives.* Premier Ebook Services, 2014.

Mann, Fred. "Wichita Boy's Garage-sale Buy Holds a Treasure for His Family." *The Wichita Eagle.* Published May 25, 2012; Updated March 6, 2014.

Mills, R. *While Out of My Body I Saw God, Hell, and the Living Dead!*, second edition. Triunity Publishing, 2007.

Nehale, Victoria. *A Friendly Reminder: Time is Fast Running Out!* Author-Publishers, 2008.

Pfeiffer, Eric. "Emails from dead man's account helping family and friends find closure." Blog. March 14, 2012. http://news.yahoo.com/blogs/sideshow/emails-dead-man-account-helping-family-friends-closure-193306965.html.

Randles, Jenny and Peter Hough. *The Afterlife: An Investigation into Life after Death*. London: BCA, 1993, reprinted 1995.

Rubin Stuart, Nancy. *The Reluctant Spiritualist: The Life of Maggie Fox*. Harcourt, 2005.

Saunders, Fr. William P. "Straight Answers: What Is Purgatory Like?" *Catholic Herald*. November 17, 2005. http://catholicherald.com/stories/Straight-Answers-What-Is-Purgatory-Like,2001?sub_id=2001.

Storm, Howard. *My Descent Into Death: A Second Chance at Life*. Harmony, 2005.

Voell, Paula. "Visitations." *The Buffalo News* (Buffalo, NY). May 27, 2001.

Weisberg, Barbara. *Talking to the Dead: Kate and Maggie Fox and the Rise of Spiritualism*. Harper San Francisco, 2004.

Weiss, Bill. *23 Minutes In Hell: One Man's Story About What He Saw, Heard, and Felt in that Place of Torment*, first edition. Charisma House, 2006.

Wills-Brandon, Carla. *One Last Hug Before I Go*. Health Communications, Inc., 2000.

Wortman, Camille B. and Elizabeth F. Loftus. *Psychology*. Knopf, 1981.

Photo By E.C. Campbell Photography

About the Author

Kristy Robinett is a psychic medium and author who began seeing spirits at the age of three. When she was eight, the spirit of her deceased grandfather helped her escape from a would-be kidnapper, and it was then that Robinett realized the Other Side wasn't so far away.

As an adult, she was often called upon by the local police department to examine cold cases in a new light and from a different angle. She gained a solid reputation for being extremely accurate at psychical profiling and giving new perspectives on unsolved crimes. It was then that she began working with a variety of law enforcement agencies, attorneys, and private investigators around the United States, aiding in missing persons, arson, and cold cases. In 2014 she appeared on a one-hour special on the Investigation Discovery Network (ID), "Restless Souls," spotlighting a police case she assisted on.

Robinett teaches psychic development and paranormal investigating at local colleges, lectures across the country, and is a regular media commentator. She is the author of *It's a*

Wonderful Afterlife; Forevermore: Guided in Spirit by Edgar Allan Poe; Messenger Between Worlds: True Stories from a Psychic Medium; Higher Intuitions Oracle; Ghosts of Southeast Michigan; and *Michigan's Haunted Legends and Lore.*

Kristy Robinett is a wife and mom to four kids and several animals. She enjoys gardening, cooking, and exploring old country towns. Her dream is to one day purchase and restore a hundred-plus-year-old farmhouse, ghosts and spirits optional.

You can visit her online at KristyRobinett.com, facebook.com/kristyrobinett, or Twitter.com/kristyrobinett.